Essential Slow Cooker Recipes

Also in This Series

Family Favorite Casserole Recipes:
103 Comforting Breakfast Casseroles, Dinner Ideas,
and Desserts Everyone Will Love

No-Bake Desserts:
103 Easy Recipes for No-Bake Cookies, Bars, and Treats

Everyday Dinner Ideas:
103 Easy Recipes for Chicken, Pasta, and
Other Dishes Everyone Will Love

Easy Cookie Recipes:
103 Best Recipes for Chocolate Chip Cookies, Cake Mix Creations,
Bars, and Holiday Treats Everyone Will Love

Retro Recipes from the '50s and '60s:
103 Vintage Appetizers, Dinners, and Drinks Everyone Will Love

Essential Slow Cooker Recipes

*103 Fuss-Free Slow Cooker Meals
Everyone Will Love*

Addie Gundry

St. Martin's Griffin ✖ New York

ESSENTIAL SLOW COOKER RECIPES. Text and photos copyright © 2017 Prime Publishing, LLC. All rights reserved. Printed in the United States of America. For information, address St. Martin's Press, 175 Fifth Avenue, New York, N.Y. 10010.

www.stmartins.com

Photography by Megan Von Schönhoff and Tom Krawczyk

The Library of Congress Cataloging-in-Publication Data is available upon request.

ISBN 978-1-250-12338-1 (trade paperback)
ISBN 978-1-250-12339-8 (ebook)

Our books may be purchased in bulk for promotional, educational, or business use. Please contact your local bookseller or the Macmillan Corporate and Premium Sales Department at 1-800-221-7945, extension 5442, or by email at MacmillanSpecialMarkets@macmillan.com.

First Edition: January 2018

10 9 8 7 6 5 4 3 2 1

To my dad.
Thank you for teaching me
patience and kindness, and for your
continuous love and support.

Contents

Introduction   1

1
Appetizer Recipes

Bacon Cheeseburger Dip   5

Bacon-Wrapped Smokies   6

Barbecue Meatballs   9

Beer and Brown Sugar Kielbasa   10

Buffalo Wings   13

Parmesan Ranch Oyster Crackers   14

Sweet-and-Savory Party Mix   17

Queso Blanco   18

Honey Buffalo Chicken Sliders   21

Shredded Chicken Nachos   22

7-Layer Dip   25

Spinach Artichoke Dip   26

2
Breakfast Recipes

Banana French Toast   31

Blueberry Breakfast Casserole   32

Sausage and Hash Brown Casserole   35

Chocolate Chip French Toast   36

Cinnamon Rolls   39

Coffee Cake   40

Easy Quiche   43

Veggie Omelet   44

Potato Puff Breakfast Casserole   47

Chocolate Chip Banana Bread   48

Easy Artisan Bread   51

Lemon Poppy Seed Bread   52

Monkey Bread   55

3
Classic Recipes

Beef Stroganoff   59

Chicken Parmesan   60

Chili   63

Buffalo Chicken Sandwiches   64

Corned Beef and Cabbage   67

4-Cheese Vegetarian Eggplant Parmesan   68

From-Scratch Italian Lasagna   71

Ritz Cracker Meat Loaf   72

Chicken Cordon Bleu   75

Melt-in-Your-Mouth Pot Roast   76

Pulled Pork   79

Sweet Sesame Ribs   80

Roasted Chicken   83

Smothered Pork Chops in Mushroom Sauce   84

Stuffed Peppers   87

Lemon Pepper Chicken Breasts   88

Tuna Casserole   91

4
Dinner Recipes

Baked Ziti   95

French Dip Sandwiches   96

Sweet Pineapple Ham   99

Ham and Cheese Potatoes   100

Jambalaya   103

Potato Puff Casserole   104

Caesar Chicken   107

Cheesy Chicken and Rice   108

Chicken Broccoli Alfredo   111

Philly Cheesesteaks   112

Pierogi Casserole with Sausage   115

Bourbon Chicken   116

Soba Noodles with Vegetables   119

Slow Cooker Pork Chops   120

General Tso's Chicken   123

Mississippi Chicken   124

Orange Chicken   127

Ranch Bacon Chicken Dinner   128

French Onion Pork Chops   131

Slow Cooker Chicken Breast with Stuffing   132

6-Ingredient Sriracha Chicken   135

Beef and Broccoli   136

Chicken Fried Rice   139

Honey Mustard Chicken and Broccoli   140

Lemon Pepper Salmon   143

Shredded Chicken Tacos   144

Teriyaki Chicken   147

5
Side Dish Recipes

Au Gratin Potatoes   151

DIY Baked Potatoes   152

Buttery Corn on the Cob   155

Creamed Corn   156

Creamy Mashed Potatoes   159

Honey-Glazed Carrots   160

Country-Style Baked Beans   163

Mac 'n' Cheese   164

Slow Cooker Stuffing   167

Corn Bread   168

Pizza Pull-Apart Bread   171

Dinner Rolls   172

6
Soup and Stew Recipes

French Onion Soup   177

Chicken Noodle Soup   178

Chicken Tortilla Soup   181

Budget-Friendly Chicken Stew   182

Cheeseburger Soup   185

Minestrone Pasta   186

Hungarian Goulash   189

Potato Soup   190

Hearty Beef Stew   193

Taco Soup   194

7
Dessert Recipes

Dump Cake   199

Apple Dumplings   200

Apple Pecan Bread Pudding   203

Berry Crumble   204

Caramel Blondies   207

Gluten-Free Zucchini Bread   208

Pineapple Upside-Down Cake   211

Hot Fudge Brownies   212

Peach Cobbler   215

Peanut Butter Cup Cake   216

Old-Fashioned Pecan Pie   219

Pumpkin Cake   220

Acknowledgments   222

Index   223

About the Author   228

Introduction

We all know that slow cooker recipes are the perfect solution for a busy day, the best way to avoid dish duty, a shortcut to adding a comforting smell to your home, and an oven-free dinner hack in the hot summer heat. The list goes on, but I'm also here to bust the myth that slow cookers are only for making stews and chilies. We've changed things up when it comes to slow-cooked food. These recipes tackle everything from breads to omelets to nachos and are as simple as you might expect, but with a little love and a few sauces and garnishes, they will look like they came from a five-star restaurant.

When the weather starts to change from hot summer nights to cooler fall days, I am always eager to change the way I eat. Don't get me wrong—I could certainly grill year-round and I love the fresh berries that summer brings, but there is something warm and cozy about making that first batch of Chicken Noodle Soup (page 178), inviting friends over for football on Sunday and serving Pulled Pork (page 79), or making memories with friends over a pot of Chili (page 63) and slice of Corn Bread (page 168). Not to mention, the slow cooker allows me to keep my oven off in the summer, so I'm not heating up the entire house just making dinner.

When I was gathering together my favorite slow cooker recipes, it was hard to stop at 100. When you come to our house, we want you to know you can always bring a friend, or two, or three. One hundred felt so rigid, and similar to the guest count on game night, or the number of helpings my husband serves himself when the house fills with the smell of a slow-cooked meal, there is always room for three more.

I invite you to dive in and enjoy the ease that a slow cooker meal brings, without compromising the taste or the beauty. Each one of these dishes, whether fresh bread or a hearty breakfast, is as delicious as it is elegant, without the fuss!

—Addie Gundry

1

Appetizer Recipes

Guests are on their way, but you still have errands to run before everyone arrives. As you're bustling about trying to balance making phone calls with hanging up decorations, throwing together a last-minute appetizer shouldn't even be on your radar. Prep one or two of these easy recipes in the morning before things get crazy, and you'll have worry-free eats that are hot and ready just in time for company to arrive.

Bacon Cheeseburger Dip

Yield: Serves 8 to 10 | Prep Time: 20 minutes | Cook Time: 2 hours

The classic combination of bacon and cheese makes this dip a cozy and filling crowd-pleaser for sporting events. Boasting the taste of a cheeseburger, but in party form, this dip reminds me of Saturdays in the fall with my husband and his friends. Keep napkins handy, because this one might get a bit messy.

INGREDIENTS

4 lean bacon slices, plus extra for garnish

1 pound lean ground beef or turkey

1 (8-ounce) package cream cheese, cut into cubes

2 cups shredded cheddar cheese

1 (14.5-ounce) can diced tomatoes, slightly drained

2 tablespoons sweet pickle relish

1 tablespoon yellow mustard

1 tablespoon ketchup

Pita chips, for dipping

DIRECTIONS

1. Spray the insert of a 6-quart slow cooker with cooking spray.

2. Cook the bacon until crisp. Drain on paper towels and crumble.

3. In a large skillet, stir the ground beef over medium-high heat for about 3 minutes until lightly browned—if the beef or turkey is not entirely cooked, don't worry. It will finish in the slow cooker. Drain well.

4. Return the meat to the hot skillet and stir in the cream cheese until melted. Add the cheddar cheese and stir to combine. Add the tomatoes, sweet pickle relish, mustard, and ketchup and stir until combined.

5. Pour the mixture into the prepared slow cooker, cover, and cook on Low for 2 hours. Turn off the slow cooker, uncover, and stir.

6. Serve in a bowl directly from the slow cooker, which will keep the mixture hot and dippable for up to 3 hours. Garnish with the bacon bits.

Bacon-Wrapped Smokies

Yield: 36 smokies | Prep Time: 20 minutes | Cook Time: 3 hours

Whether you call them a baconized version of Pigs in a Blanket or, my personal favorite, Bacon-Wrapped Smokies, there's no denying how addicting these are! It's the sweet-and-salty combination of maple syrup and bacon that really sells the dish. It also happens to be my go-to for a hearty brunch.

INGREDIENTS

1¾ cups packed dark brown sugar

1 (12-ounce) package bacon

1 (14-ounce) package cocktail links

¼ cup maple syrup

1 tablespoon Dijon mustard

Pinch of cayenne pepper

DIRECTIONS

1. Sprinkle 1 cup of the brown sugar over the bottom of a 6-quart slow cooker.

2. Cut the bacon into thirds crosswise.

3. Wrap a strip of bacon around each of the cocktail links. It's easier to wrap if the bacon is cold.

4. Poke a 6-inch wooden skewer through 5 or 6 Bacon-Wrapped Smokies to hold the bacon in place. Repeat with the remaining smokies.

5. Place the smokies into the slow cooker over the brown sugar.

6. In a small bowl, whisk together the maple syrup, Dijon mustard, and cayenne. Drizzle the mixture over the smokies, then sprinkle the remaining ¾ cup of brown sugar over the top.

7. Cover and cook on High for 3 hours or until the bacon is cooked, flipping the smokies over 3 or 4 times during cooking.

8. If you want the bacon to be crispy, remove the smokies from the slow cooker and place them on a foil-lined baking sheet, then broil for about 5 minutes. Leave them on the skewers to serve or remove and stick individual toothpicks through each smokie for larger crowds.

Barbecue Meatballs

Yield: 48 meatballs | Prep Time: 25 minutes | Cook Time: 5 hours

Have those toothpicks and fancy swords at the ready! These party-worthy meatballs are sure to get gobbled up before you know it. My favorite part about them is that I can make a batch for an appetizer one night and serve them on top of a heaping plate of spaghetti the next.

INGREDIENTS

Sauce

1 tablespoon olive oil

1 cup onion, very finely chopped

1 garlic clove, finely minced

1 (15-ounce) can tomato sauce

½ cup red wine vinegar

½ cup packed light brown sugar

⅓ cup chili sauce

2 tablespoons Worcestershire sauce

½ (1-ounce) packet dry French onion soup mix (about 2 tablespoons)

1 teaspoon liquid smoke

Meatballs

¼ cup whole milk

1 large egg

1 cup coarse bread crumbs (made from sliced whole-wheat bread)

1 pound lean ground beef or a combination of beef and pork

½ (1-ounce) packet dry French onion soup mix (about 2 tablespoons)

1 teaspoon Worcestershire sauce

Scallions, sliced, for garnish

DIRECTIONS

1. *For the sauce:* In a medium skillet, heat the oil over medium heat. Add the onion and garlic and cook, stirring frequently, until the onion is translucent. Add the tomato sauce and bring to a simmer while adding the vinegar, brown sugar, chili sauce, Worcestershire sauce, onion soup mix, and liquid smoke. Pour into a 6-quart slow cooker, cover, and cook on Low while mixing the meatballs.

2. *For the meatballs:* Combine the milk and egg in a medium bowl. Add the bread crumbs and soak for 5 minutes. Stir in the beef, onion soup mix, and Worcestershire sauce. Mix very well.

3. Use a tablespoon to portion the mixture, rolling between your palms to a golf ball size. As you make the balls, immediately drop them into the slow cooker with the sauce. When all the balls are formed, stir very gently, just enough to get the top pieces coated in sauce, then cover and cook on Low for 5 hours.

4. The meatballs and sauce can be made ahead, removed from the slow cooker, and cooled completely. Store in a covered container in the refrigerator. When you're ready to eat them, return the meatballs and sauce to the slow cooker, cover, and reheat on High until warmed through. Garnish with scallions.

Beer and Brown Sugar Kielbasa

Yield: Serves 8 | Prep Time: 10 minutes | Cook Time: 4 hours

Last Christmas my husband was given a kegerator system for our basement bar! It has become my go-to for beer-inspired recipes, and this is one of my new favorites. The beer helps tenderize and bring out the flavor of the meat, so you don't even need to add any extra spices. The sauerkraut adds a distinct tang to contrast with the brown sugar.

INGREDIENTS

28 ounces kielbasa

18–20 ounces sauerkraut, drained and rinsed

1 cup packed dark brown sugar

1 (12-ounce) can of beer

8 buns, for serving (optional)

DIRECTIONS

1. Spray the insert of a 6-quart slow cooker with cooking spray.

2. Slice the kielbasa into 3- to 3½-inch links and place in the slow cooker.

3. Cover the kielbasa with the sauerkraut.

4. Sprinkle the brown sugar over the sauerkraut, then pour the beer over all.

5. Cover and cook on High for 4 hours.

6. Serve as is or on buns.

NOTES

You can substitute store-bought ranch dressing for the homemade ranch dipping sauce, if you wish.

Buffalo Wings

Yield: Serves 8 | Prep Time: 1 hour | Cook Time: 2 hours on High, then 2 hours on Low

Football season isn't complete without homemade buffalo wings. Sticky, hot orange fingers are one of my favorite visions of winter. Messy hands, the ultimate sacrifice, are so worth it! And when served with ranch or blue cheese dressing to counter the spiciness, these are everything you need in a party snack.

INGREDIENTS

2 (12-ounce) bottles hot pepper sauce

1 cup (2 sticks) unsalted butter

2 tablespoons Worcestershire sauce

2 tablespoons honey

2 tablespoons light brown sugar

2 teaspoons dried oregano

2 teaspoons onion powder

2 teaspoons garlic powder

½ teaspoon cayenne pepper

4 pounds chicken wings

Ranch Dipping Sauce

½ cup sour cream

½ cup buttermilk

¼ cup mayonnaise

2 garlic cloves, minced

1 teaspoon dried dill

3–4 teaspoons finely chopped fresh chives

2 teaspoons fresh lemon juice

1 teaspoon kosher salt

¼ teaspoon freshly ground black pepper

DIRECTIONS

1. Spray the insert of a 6-quart slow cooker with cooking spray.

2. In a large saucepan, combine 1 bottle of hot pepper sauce, ½ cup (1 stick) of the butter, the Worcestershire sauce, honey, brown sugar, dried oregano, onion powder, garlic powder, and cayenne and bring to a boil over medium heat. Reduce the heat to low and simmer for 5 minutes.

3. Place the chicken wings in the slow cooker and pour the sauce over the wings.

4. Cook the wings on High for 2 hours. Reduce the heat to Low and cook for 2 hours more.

5. Just before the wings are done, preheat the oven to 400°F.

6. In a medium saucepan, combine the remaining bottle of hot pepper sauce and ½ cup (1 stick) butter and simmer over medium heat for 15 to 20 minutes.

7. Line two baking sheets with aluminum foil and spray with cooking spray. Place the wings on the baking sheets and cook for 20 minutes, until crispy.

8. *For the ranch dipping sauce:* In a medium bowl, whisk together the sour cream, buttermilk, mayonnaise, garlic, dill, chives, lemon juice, salt, and pepper. Chill until ready to use.

9. Brush the wings with the remaining sauce and serve with the ranch dipping sauce.

Parmesan Ranch Oyster Crackers

Yield: Serves 4 to 6 | Prep Time: 5 minutes | Cook Time: 1 hour

If you need a snack that's effortless to make, these crackers are versatile enough for any occasion. I remember making them with my grandfather when I was younger. Along with pickles, they were his signature snack that I can't make without thinking of my time in the kitchen with him. They look fancy enough to set out in a small serving bowl during a holiday party, but they're still fit for munching on on a Sunday night when you're lounging in your sweatpants.

INGREDIENTS

½ cup (1 stick) unsalted butter, melted

1 (1-ounce) package ranch dressing mix

4 garlic cloves, minced

½ teaspoon dried dill

2 (8-ounce) packages oyster crackers

¾ cup freshly grated Parmesan cheese

¼ cup chopped fresh parsley leaves

DIRECTIONS

1. Spray the insert of a 6-quart slow cooker with cooking spray.

2. In a small bowl, combine the melted butter, ranch dressing mix, garlic, and dill.

3. Put the oyster crackers in a slow cooker and pour the butter mixture over the top. Stir to combine and coat the crackers. Cover and cook on Low, stirring occasionally, for 1 hour. Remove the crackers from the slow cooker and place in a single layer on a baking sheet. Sprinkle the Parmesan and parsley on top and stir. Let cool completely. Pour into a bowl and serve.

Sweet-and-Savory Party Mix

Yield: Serves 6 to 8 | Prep Time: 10 minutes | Cook Time: 3 hours

Everyone has their favorite ingredient in the party mix. Mine, of course, is the pretzel. Pretzels have always been one of my favorite foods, but you don't have to follow my lead. Party mixes are so much fun to customize to your taste. Replace the cashews with pecans. Add a little extra cinnamon. It's your party—make a mix you're sure to love!

INGREDIENTS

8 cups various cereals (I used equal parts Corn, Rice, and Wheat Chex.)

2 cups pretzels

1 cup cashews

1 cup peanuts

1 cup honey sesame sticks

¾ cup (1½ sticks) unsalted butter, melted

½ cup maple syrup

1 tablespoon kosher salt

1 tablespoon ground cinnamon

2 garlic cloves, minced

DIRECTIONS

1. Lightly spray the insert of a 6-quart slow cooker with cooking spray.

2. Put the cereal, pretzels, cashews, peanuts, and honey sesame sticks in the slow cooker.

3. In a medium bowl, whisk together the melted butter, maple syrup, salt, cinnamon, and garlic until everything is well combined. Drizzle the sauce evenly over the top of the cereal mixture. Toss for about 1 minute, or until the mixture is evenly combined.

4. Cover and cook on Low for 3 hours, stirring with a large spoon every 30 minutes. Spread the mixture out onto parchment paper in an even layer until it cools to room temperature. Serve, or store in an airtight container at room temperature for up to 10 days.

Queso Blanco

Yield: Serves 4 | Prep Time: 10 minutes | Cook Time: 45 minutes

Queso Blanco is a spicy, melty cheese dip, and it's always popular. In fact, this was a regular part of my diet while I was in high school. My girlfriends and I used to head over to a local restaurant and eat bottomless bowls of chips. Fast-forward to today and I do my best to re-create that delicious appetizer we induldged in so often. The recipe can easily be doubled, or even tripled, for a larger crowd.

INGREDIENTS

1 pound shredded mozzarella cheese

8 ounces cream cheese

1 (8.25-ounce) can creamed corn

1 tablespoon unsalted butter

1 (7-ounce) can chopped green chiles, well drained

½ teaspoon dry oregano

½ teaspoon ground cumin

Pinch of salt

1 jalapeño, seeded and finely chopped

⅓ cup heavy cream, warmed

Hot sauce, if desired

DIRECTIONS

1. Combine the mozzarella cheese, cream cheese, creamed corn, butter, green chiles, oregano, cumin, salt, and jalapeño in a 6-quart slow cooker. Cover and cook on High for 30 minutes.

2. Stir the mixture until smooth, then add the cream 1 tablespoon at a time until you reach the desired consistency. Replace the cover and cook on High for 15 minutes more. The mixture should be creamy and smooth. Taste and add hot sauce, if desired.

3. Keep the cheese dip in the slow cooker on the Warm setting until ready to serve.

NOTES

To reheat, place in the microwave with about 1 teaspoon warm water. Heat for 30 seconds, stir, add more water if needed, and repeat. The mixture thickens significantly as it cools.

Honey Buffalo Chicken Sliders

Yield: Serves 8 | Prep Time: 15 minutes | Cook Time: 4 to 5 hours

Buffalo chicken is an excellent appetizer when you have friends over, but it can be tricky to balance how spicy you ought to make a dish. The additional honey makes the spiciness much milder, so you don't have to worry about alienating anyone.

INGREDIENTS

2 pounds boneless, skinless chicken breasts (3 large or 4 small)

½ teaspoon garlic powder

½ teaspoon paprika

1 teaspoon salt

Black pepper

4 tablespoons unsalted butter

1 cup hot sauce

½ cup honey

2 tablespoons light brown sugar

2 tablespoons soy sauce

3 tablespoons ketchup

1½ tablespoons cornstarch

Rolls, for serving

Carrot and celery stalks, for serving

DIRECTIONS

1. Place the chicken in one layer in a 6-quart slow cooker and sprinkle with garlic powder, paprika, salt, and pepper. Cover and cook on Low for 4 hours.

2. Remove the chicken from the slow cooker and shred roughly with two forks.

3. In a medium bowl, combine the butter, hot sauce, honey, brown sugar, soy sauce, and ketchup.

4. Toss the chicken in the hot sauce mixture and keep warm.

5. Mix the cornstarch with 2 tablespoons of water and add to the sauce (after the chicken is removed). Simmer on high for 5 minutes, or until thickened to a syrup consistency.

6. Serve on rolls, with carrot and celery stalks alongside.

Shredded Chicken Nachos

Yield: Serves 4 | Prep Time: 5 minutes | Cook Time: 6 hours on Low or 3 hours on High

Salsa is a kitchen lifesaver, not just a pairing for chips. I make sure to have it stocked in the pantry at all times because I use it so often when cooking dinner. It makes for a wonderfully flavorful topping to a simple meal. Pick out a salsa according to your spice preference and get ready to dig in.

INGREDIENTS

4 boneless, skinless chicken breasts

1 (16-ounce) jar mild salsa

1 (10-ounce) can Ro-Tel tomatoes

½ small onion, diced

1 (13-ounce) bag tortilla chips

1 jalapeño, finely sliced

1 (2.25-ounce) can sliced black olives

1 (15-ounce) can black beans, drained

2 cups shredded Mexican four-cheese blend

½ green bell pepper, thinly sliced

Grated Oaxaca cheese, for garnish

DIRECTIONS

1. Spray the insert of a 6-quart slow cooker with cooking spray.

2. Place the chicken breasts in the slow cooker. Pour the salsa and tomatoes over the top. Sprinkle with the diced onion.

3. Cook on Low for 6 hours or on High for 3 hours. Remove the chicken from the slow cooker and shred the meat with two forks. Set aside.

4. Preheat the broiler. Layer the tortilla chips in a cast-iron dish. Top with the chicken, jalapeño, black olives, black beans, four-cheese blend, and bell pepper. Broil until the cheese is melted and bubbling, about 5 minutes.

5. Remove from the oven, top with the Oaxaca cheese, and serve.

7-Layer Dip

Yield: Serves 8 | Prep Time: 10 minutes | Cook Time: 1½ to 2 hours

Colorful and enticing, this 7-Layer Dip always takes center stage on the snack table and reminds me of a dish my dorm-mom made in school. It's so colorful and enticing that you can't look away! Make sure to serve it with chips that are large enough to scoop up each delectable layer.

INGREDIENTS

2 (15-ounce) cans chili with beans

1 (16-ounce) container sour cream

½ (8-ounce) container cream cheese, at room temperature

1 (8-ounce) package shredded Mexican-blend cheese

1 (2.25-ounce) can black olives, drained

¼ cup sliced jalapeños, jarred or fresh

2 tomatoes, seeded and diced

¼ cup sliced scallions

Corn chips or tortilla chips, for serving

DIRECTIONS

1. Spray the insert of a 6-quart slow cooker with cooking spray.

2. Spread the chili evenly over the bottom of the slow cooker.

3. In a large bowl, combine the sour cream and cream cheese and stir until well combined. Dollop the mixture over the chili, then spread it out evenly.

4. Sprinkle the Mexican-blend cheese over the top of the sour cream mixture.

5. Cover and cook on High for 1½ to 2 hours.

6. Add the black olives, jalapeños, tomatoes, and scallions in layers.

7. Serve with chips.

Spinach Artichoke Dip

Yield: Serves 6 | Prep Time: 10 minutes | Cook Time: 1½ to 2 hours

Every Christmas my mother-in-law makes her signature spinach artichoke dip, because the cousins love it! Although this dish reminds me of a special occasion, the recipe is simple enough that I can make it any day of the week.

INGREDIENTS

1 cup shredded mozzarella cheese

6 ounces cream cheese, cut into cubes

¼ cup shredded Parmesan cheese

1 garlic clove, minced

1 (14-ounce) can artichoke hearts, drained, rinsed, and finely chopped

½ cup sour cream

8 ounces baby spinach leaves

¼ teaspoon freshly ground black pepper

Crackers or tortilla chips, for dipping

DIRECTIONS

1. Spray the insert of a 6-quart slow cooker with cooking spray.

2. Combine the mozzarella, cream cheese, Parmesan, garlic, artichoke hearts, sour cream, spinach, and black pepper in the slow cooker. Stir until well combined.

3. Cover and cook on High for 1½ to 2 hours, until the dip is hot and the cheeses have melted.

4. Stir. Serve with crackers or tortilla chips.

2

Breakfast Recipes

It's said that breakfast is the most important meal of the day, but we often don't give it the attention it deserves. Breakfast is worth savoring. You don't even need to be fully awake to enjoy a slow cooker breakfast, as you would huddled over the stovetop making eggs like a short-order cook. Instead, slow cookers offer an effortless, hands-off path to the home-cooked breakfast you've been craving.

Banana French Toast

Yield: Serves 6 | Prep Time: 10 minutes | Cook Time: 4 to 5 hours on Low or 2 to 3 hours on High

You usually only see these kinds of decadent French toast recipes if you go out to Sunday brunch. I love making this as my "special occasion breakfast," when my husband gets back from a business trip or my in-laws come to visit. It's simple to make, but impressive.

INGREDIENTS

12 (1-inch-thick) slices baguette

4 large eggs

¾ cup almond milk

1 tablespoon sugar

1 tablespoon vanilla extract

1 teaspoon ground cinnamon

2 bananas, sliced

Juice of ½ lemon

2 tablespoons unsalted butter, melted

Maple syrup, for serving (optional)

DIRECTIONS

1. Spray the insert of a 6-quart slow cooker with cooking spray. Arrange the baguette slices over the bottom of the slow cooker.

2. In a medium bowl, whisk together the eggs, almond milk, sugar, vanilla, and cinnamon. Drizzle over the baguette slices, making sure to cover each slice completely with the egg mixture.

3. Put the banana slices in a medium bowl. Drizzle with the lemon juice and toss to coat. Place the banana slices on top of the baguettes in the slow cooker. Drizzle with the melted butter. Cover and cook on Low for 4 to 5 hours or on High for 2 to 3 hours, or until cooked through. Cooking times will vary with different slow cookers, so begin to check your slow cooker at the 3-hour mark on Low and the 1½-hour mark on High and cook just until the bread begins to turn golden brown around the edges.

4. Drizzle lightly with maple syrup, if desired, and serve.

Blueberry Breakfast Casserole

Yield: Serves 6 | Prep Time: 10 minutes | Cook Time: 2 hours

This made-from-scratch casserole is so easy to throw together that you can prep it quickly and then head back to bed while it cooks. When you wake up, the house will be filled with the heavenly aroma of blueberries and almonds.

INGREDIENTS

1 cup old-fashioned (not quick-cooking) oats

1 cup cream of wheat

1 cup all-purpose flour

1 cup packed light brown sugar

1 tablespoon baking powder

1 teaspoon kosher salt

1 large egg

1 cup whole milk

½ cup fresh orange juice

¼ cup vegetable oil

2 cups fresh or thawed frozen blueberries

1 tablespoon orange zest

1 cup sliced almonds

Yogurt, for topping (optional)

DIRECTIONS

1. Spray the insert of a 6-quart slow cooker with cooking spray.

2. In a large bowl, combine the oats, cream of wheat, flour, brown sugar, baking powder, and salt and stir.

3. In another medium bowl, beat the egg. Add the milk, orange juice, and vegetable oil and mix to combine. Stir the egg mixture into the oat mixture until all the dry ingredients are completely moistened. Fold in the blueberries, orange zest, and almonds. Pour the batter into the slow cooker, cover, and cook on High for 2 hours—the center may still be slightly soft.

4. Serve immediately while warm or spoon into individual containers for an easy breakfast on the go. Rewarm in the microwave for 30 seconds on high and top with plain yogurt, if desired.

Sausage and Hash Brown Casserole

Yield: Serves 10 to 12 | Prep Time: 20 minutes | Cook Time: 7 to 8 hours on Low or 3½ to 4 hours on High

It's the holidays, and you have seemingly everyone in the family crashing in the guest room, on the couch, and in every other nook and cranny of your house. When you face the daunting task of feeding breakfast to a crowd, this company-size casserole is here to bail you out.

INGREDIENTS

8 ounces shredded cheddar cheese

8 ounces shredded Colby Jack cheese

1 (26–30-ounce) bag frozen hash browns

1 small onion, chopped

1 pound breakfast sausage, cooked and drained

10 large eggs

½ cup half-and-half

½ teaspoon kosher salt

½ teaspoon freshly ground black pepper

DIRECTIONS

1. Lightly spray the insert of a 6-quart slow cooker with cooking spray.

2. In a medium bowl, combine the cheddar and Colby Jack cheeses.

3. Place one-third of the hash browns over the bottom of the slow cooker. Top with one-third of the onion, then one-third of the cheese mixture, and then one-third of the breakfast sausage. Repeat the layers twice.

4. In a large bowl, whisk together the eggs, half-and-half, salt, and pepper.

5. Pour the mixture over the top.

6. Cook on Low for 7 to 8 hours or on High for 3½ to 4 hours, until the eggs are set.

7. Cut into squares and serve.

Chocolate Chip French Toast

Yield: Serves 6 to 8 | Prep Time: 15 minutes, plus 4 hours chill time
Cook Time: 4 hours on Low or 2 hours on High

Guess what? Challah bread is the key to making the sweetest French toast. This is one of the best kept secrets and will make you the star of the kitchen. I like serving this with whipped cream, but you could also add fresh fruit, like sliced strawberries, or chocolate syrup if you want to make this an extra-special treat.

INGREDIENTS

1 (1-pound) loaf challah bread, thickly sliced

¾ cup semisweet or dark chocolate chips

3 large eggs

1½ cups heavy cream

¾ cup packed light brown sugar

1 teaspoon vanilla extract or vanilla bean paste

1 teaspoon ground cinnamon

Whipped cream (optional)

DIRECTIONS

1. Lightly spray the insert of a 6-quart slow cooker with cooking spray.

2. Layer half the bread slices over the bottom of the slow cooker.

3. Sprinkle half the chocolate chips over the bread slices.

4. Layer the remaining bread slices on top of the chocolate chips.

5. In a small bowl, whisk together the eggs, cream, brown sugar, vanilla, and cinnamon.

6. Pour the egg mixture over the bread slices. Gently press down on the slices to submerge.

7. Sprinkle the remaining chocolate chips on top.

8. Cover, remove the insert, and refrigerate for 4 hours.

9. Let the insert sit out on the counter for 15 minutes. Replace the insert and cook on Low for 4 hours or on High for 2 hours.

10. Serve with whipped cream, if desired.

VARIATIONS

Use French bread or croissants in place of the challah.

Cinnamon Rolls

Yield: Serves 6 to 8 | Prep Time: 35 minutes | Cook Time: 2 hours

You can't go wrong with homemade cinnamon rolls, and I'll tell you what—you can make and eat them any time of day! With a warm, gooey, fall-apart-in-your-mouth center and smooth, creamy frosting on top, there's no better way to start the morning or enjoy an afternoon break.

INGREDIENTS

Cinnamon Rolls

¾ cup whole milk, lukewarm

1 (0.25-ounce) packet instant yeast

¼ cup granulated sugar

1 teaspoon kosher salt

3 tablespoons unsalted butter, melted

1 large egg

2¾ cups all-purpose flour

Filling

2 tablespoons ground cinnamon

½ cup granulated sugar

1 cup chopped pecans

5 tablespoons unsalted butter, at room temperature

Cream Cheese Frosting

1¼ cups powdered sugar

2 ounces cream cheese

2 tablespoons whole milk

1 teaspoon vanilla extract

DIRECTIONS

1. *For the cinnamon rolls:* Pour the warm milk into the bowl of a stand mixer and add the yeast and 1 teaspoon of the granulated sugar. Stir lightly. Set aside until the yeast is foamy, 5 to 10 minutes.

2. Fit the mixer with the paddle attachment. On low speed, beat in the remaining granulated sugar. Add the salt, butter, egg, and 2 cups of the flour and mix until combined. With the mixer running on low speed, add the remaining ¾ cup flour, ¼ cup at a time, until a soft dough forms and the dough starts to pull away from the sides of the bowl. Beat on low speed for 2 minutes more to knead the dough. Cover the bowl of the mixer with a clean dish towel and let rest for 15 minutes.

3. *For the filling:* Prepare the slow cooker by lining the inside with parchment paper and spraying with cooking spray.

4. In a small bowl, combine the cinnamon, granulated sugar, and pecans.

5. Turn the dough out onto a board and roll it out to an 8 × 14–inch rectangle. Spread the softened butter on top. Sprinkle the cinnamon mixture evenly over the dough.

6. Roll the dough tightly starting from one long edge, then slice it crosswise into 10 even pieces. Arrange the rolls inside the lined slow cooker. Place a long piece of paper towel over the top of the slow cooker and cover with the lid.

7. Cook on High for 2 hours. Once the rolls are completely cooked, transfer them to a serving platter by lifting out the parchment paper.

8. *For the cream cheese frosting:* In a small bowl, whisk together the powdered sugar, cream cheese, milk, and vanilla until smooth. Drizzle over the warm rolls and serve immediately.

Coffee Cake

Yield: Serves 6 to 8 | Prep Time: 15 minutes | Cook Time: 1½ to 2 hours

Brew up a steaming pot of fresh coffee to pair with this sweet, cinnamon-rich coffee cake. The cardamom is my secret ingredient, and helps make this the perfect recipe for slow-cooked deliciousness. Plus, your house is going to smell divine.

INGREDIENTS

3½ cups biscuit baking mix

1½ cups granulated sugar

1 cup sour cream

2 large eggs, beaten

2 teaspoons vanilla extract

2 apples, peeled, cored, and diced

½ cup packed light brown sugar

1 teaspoon ground cinnamon

¼ teaspoon ground cardamom

1 cup powdered sugar

2–4 tablespoons heavy cream or milk

DIRECTIONS

1. Spray the insert of a 6-quart slow cooker with cooking spray.

2. Line the slow cooker with a large piece of parchment paper covering the bottom and up the sides about 4 inches. (You can trace the slow cooker lid to get the size of the bottom of the slow cooker, then add 4 inches.)

3. In a medium bowl, combine the biscuit baking mix, granulated sugar, sour cream, eggs, vanilla, and apples.

4. In a small bowl, mix the brown sugar, cinnamon, and cardamom.

5. Pour half the apple mixture into the slow cooker and spread it into an even layer over the bottom.

6. Sprinkle half the brown sugar mixture over the batter.

7. Top with the remainder of the apple mixture, then the remaining brown sugar mixture.

8. Place two long pieces of paper towel over the top of the slow cooker and cover with the lid.

9. Cover and cook on High for 1½ to 2 hours, until the batter has set and a toothpick inserted into the center comes out clean.

10. Remove the lid and let the coffee cake sit for 10 minutes.

11. Carefully pull up on the parchment to lift the coffee cake out.

12. In a small bowl, mix together the powdered sugar with the cream. Drizzle over the coffee cake. Cut into squares and serve.

Easy Quiche

Yield: Serves 10 | Prep Time: 20 minutes | Cook Time: 3 to 4 hours

Quiche can seem intimidating, but this simple slow cooker dish will prove that it's not at all. The rolled-out piecrust is a great time-saver, since you don't have to worry about making it from scratch.

INGREDIENTS

2 (9-inch) prepared piecrusts, rolled out

1 teaspoon olive oil

½ cup diced shallots

1 garlic clove, minced

9 large eggs

1¼ cups heavy cream

½ teaspoon kosher salt

¼ teaspoon freshly ground black pepper

⅛ teaspoon freshly grated nutmeg

10 bacon slices, cooked and chopped

2 cups baby spinach, chopped

8 ounces Gruyère cheese, shredded

Chopped fresh chives, for garnish

DIRECTIONS

1. Spray the insert of a 6-quart slow cooker with cooking spray.

2. Place an 18-inch piece of parchment paper on the counter. Place the two rolled-out piecrusts on the parchment paper, overlapping the dough in the center to create one large piece. Lightly press the dough together. Carefully pick up the dough with the parchment paper and place it into the slow cooker. Press the dough into the edges of the slow cooker, then up the sides by 2½ to 3 inches; crimp the dough to fit.

3. In a small sauté pan, heat the olive oil over medium heat. Add the shallots and garlic and cook for 3 to 4 minutes, until slightly softened.

4. In a large bowl, whisk together the eggs, cream, salt, pepper, and nutmeg. Add the shallots and garlic and mix.

5. Sprinkle half the bacon, spinach, and Gruyère over the crust in the slow cooker.

6. Pour half the egg mixture evenly over the ingredients in the slow cooker. Top with the rest of the bacon, spinach, and Gruyère, then the remaining egg mixture.

7. Place a long piece of paper towel over the top of the slow cooker and cover with the lid.

8. Cook on High for 3 to 4 hours, until the quiche is set and the crust is golden brown.

9. Carefully lift the edges of the parchment paper to remove the quiche.

10. Sprinkle with chopped chives, slice, and serve.

Veggie Omelet

Yield: Serves 4 to 6 | Prep Time: 15 minutes | Cook Time: 1½ to 2 hours

I love heading out to the farmers' market to see what produce is in season. The offerings are always so juicy and colorful that I tend to go a little overboard. Recipes like this Veggie Omelet save the day.

INGREDIENTS

1 cup chopped zucchini

1 cup sliced cremini mushrooms

1 red bell pepper, julienned

1–2 small shallots, diced

1 garlic clove, minced

6 large eggs

½ cup whole milk

¼ teaspoon kosher salt

¼ teaspoon freshly ground black pepper

¼ teaspoon red pepper flakes

¼ teaspoon herbes de Provence

1 cup shredded cheddar cheese

1 tomato, chopped, for garnish

3 scallions, chopped, for garnish

Sour cream, for garnish

DIRECTIONS

1. Lightly spray the insert of a 6-quart slow cooker with cooking spray.

2. Add the zucchini, mushrooms, bell pepper, shallots, and garlic to the slow cooker and mix.

3. In a large bowl, combine the eggs, milk, salt, black pepper, red pepper flakes, and herbes de Provence and whisk until well mixed.

4. Pour the egg mixture over the vegetables in the slow cooker and stir to combine.

5. Cover and cook on High for 1½ to 2 hours, until the eggs are set; start checking after 1½ hours.

6. Sprinkle the cheese over the omelet and cook on High for 2 to 3 minutes more, until the cheese has melted.

7. Cut the omelet into wedges and serve garnished with tomato, scallions, and sour cream.

Potato Puff Breakfast Casserole

Yield: Serves 8 | Prep Time: 10 minutes | Cook Time: 4 hours on Low or 2 hours on High

I grew up in Minnesota, and potato puffs were a big part of my diet as a kid. So take it from me: If you ever have trouble getting your kids to sit down for breakfast, this recipe will be a lifesaver. Just tell them the dish has potato puffs in it, and they'll be scrambling to find a spot at the table.

INGREDIENTS

2 tablespoons olive oil

1 pound ground turkey

¾ cup finely chopped onion

1 teaspoon minced garlic

6 large eggs

¼ cup sour cream

½ teaspoon red pepper flakes (optional)

½ teaspoon kosher salt

¼ teaspoon freshly ground black pepper

1 (32-ounce) package frozen potato puffs

1 cup shredded sharp cheddar cheese

2 tablespoons chopped fresh parsley, plus extra for garnish, if desired

DIRECTIONS

1. Spray the insert of a 6-quart slow cooker with cooking spray.

2. In a large nonstick skillet, heat the olive oil over medium-high heat. Add the turkey and onion and cook, stirring frequently, for 3 minutes, until the turkey begins to brown. Add the garlic and cook, stirring, for 1 to 2 minutes more.

3. While the turkey cooks, in a medium bowl whisk together the eggs, sour cream, red pepper flakes (if using), salt, and black pepper.

4. Arrange half the potato puffs in a single layer over the bottom of the slow cooker. Spoon the turkey mixture on top, then pour the eggs over the turkey. Add the remaining potato puffs in a single layer and top evenly with the cheese and parsley.

5. Cover and cook on Low for 4 hours or on High for 2 hours.

6. Garnish with parsley, if desired, and serve.

Chocolate Chip Banana Bread

Yield: Serves 4-6 | Prep Time: 20 minutes | Cook Time: 2½ hours

How often do you buy too many bananas and have to throw them out because they go bad? The next time you run into this dilemma, bake up this Chocolate Chip Banana Bread instead. Brown bananas make the center so moist and mouthwatering that you may start letting bananas go brown on purpose.

INGREDIENTS

½ cup (1 stick) unsalted butter, softened

2 large eggs

1 cup sugar

2 cups all-purpose flour

1 teaspoon baking powder

½ teaspoon baking soda

½ teaspoon kosher salt

4 bananas, mashed

1 cup semisweet chocolate chunks

⅓ cup mini semisweet chocolate chips

DIRECTIONS

1. Spray a 6-quart slow cooker with cooking spray. In a large bowl, combine the butter, eggs, and sugar.

2. Add the flour, baking powder, baking soda, and salt and mix well.

3. Add the mashed bananas and stir until combined.

4. Add the chocolate chunks.

5. Pour the mixture inside the slow cooker, cover, and cook on Low for 2½ hours. Remove and top with the mini chocolate chips. Serve.

Easy Artisan Bread

Yield: 8 slices | Prep Time: 15 minutes | Cook Time: 1½ hours

I couldn't believe it was possible to make delicious bread in a slow cooker, but now I'm completely converted, and this is my favorite bread recipe around. You'll be amazed at how soft and airy the texture is, as if you've purchased the bread fresh from a bakery.

INGREDIENTS

1 cup warm water

1 tablespoon quick-rise yeast

1 tablespoon honey

2¾ cups all-purpose flour

1 tablespoon sugar

1 teaspoon kosher salt

2 tablespoons olive oil

DIRECTIONS

1. In a small bowl, mix together the warm (not hot) water, yeast, and honey and let sit for a minute for the yeast to foam.

2. In a large bowl, combine the flour, sugar, and salt, then mix with the yeast mixture and olive oil, stirring with a wooden spoon until the dough comes together.

3. Knead the dough for 5 minutes, either by hand or in the bowl of a stand mixer and fitted with the dough hook. Form the dough into a large ball.

4. Line the insert of a 6-quart slow cooker with parchment paper and place the dough ball in the center.

5. Place a long piece of paper towel over the top of the slow cooker and cover with the lid, leaving it very slightly ajar. This will help absorb some of the moisture so the top of your bread doesn't turn out mushy and wet and the bottom crispy and hard.

6. Cook on High for 1½ hours, or until the bottom of the bread browns. (You can just lift it out with the parchment to check how brown the bottom is.)

7. Preheat the oven to broil. Remove the bread from the slow cooker and put it on a baking sheet. Broil for 2 to 3 minutes, or until it is the desired golden brown. Let the bread cool for 5 minutes before slicing and serving.

Lemon Poppy Seed Bread

Yield: Serves 6 to 8 | Prep Time: 20 minutes | Cook Time: 1½ to 2 hours

The lemon in my go-to brunch bread gives it a bright, sunny quality that wakes you up on a sleepy morning and pairs nicely with coffee or tea, while the poppy seeds add a welcome crunch. It's one of my favorite muffins turned into bread, and I can't get enough of it!

INGREDIENTS

Bread

2 cups all-purpose flour

¼ cup yellow cornmeal

¼ cup poppy seeds

1 tablespoon baking powder

½ teaspoon kosher salt

1 cup granulated sugar

3 large eggs

½ cup vegetable oil

½ cup plain Greek yogurt or sour cream

¼ cup whole milk

1 teaspoon lemon zest

¼ cup fresh lemon juice

1 teaspoon vanilla extract

Glaze

½ cup powdered sugar

1 teaspoon lemon zest

1½ tablespoons fresh lemon juice

DIRECTIONS

1. *For the bread:* Line the bottom and sides of a 6-quart slow cooker with parchment paper. Lightly spray the parchment with cooking spray.

2. In a large bowl, combine the flour, cornmeal, poppy seeds, baking powder, and salt.

3. In another large bowl, whisk together the granulated sugar, eggs, vegetable oil, yogurt, milk, lemon zest, lemon juice, and vanilla.

4. Add the sugar mixture to the flour mixture and stir until just combined.

5. Spoon the batter into the slow cooker. Cover and cook on high for 1½ to 2 hours, until the center is set. Start checking at 1½ hours. Once the bread is set, turn off the slow cooker.

6. Carefully lift the cover and place a long piece of paper towel over the top of the slow cooker. Place the lid back on and let cool for 10 to 15 minutes.

7. Lift the bread from the slow cooker and place on a wire rack.

8. *For the glaze:* Combine the powdered sugar, lemon zest, and lemon juice until well mixed and drizzle over the top of the bread. Cut into slices and serve.

Monkey Bread

Yield: Serves 8 | Prep Time: 15 minutes | Cook Time: 2 to 2½ hours

Monkey Bread is always a hit with kids. They love that it's gooey, sticky, and sweet. Feel free to play around with this recipe. If you love pecans, go ahead and add those too. Grabbed a few extra apples at the grocery store? Slice 'em up and put those in, right between the pieces of dough.

INGREDIENTS

½ cup granulated sugar

½ cup packed light brown sugar

½ (8-ounce) package cream cheese

1 teaspoon ground cinnamon

½ cup (1 stick) unsalted butter

1 (16.3-ounce) tube Pillsbury Grands refrigerated rolls

DIRECTIONS

1. Spray the insert of a 6-quart slow cooker with cooking spray. Line the slow cooker with a large piece of parchment paper covering the bottom and up the sides about 4 inches. (You can trace the slow cooker lid to get the size of the bottom of the slow cooker, then add 4 inches.)

2. In a large bowl or zip-top plastic bag, combine the granulated sugar and brown sugar. Unwrap the cream cheese and sprinkle with ½ teaspoon of the cinnamon; add the remaining ½ teaspoon cinnamon to the container with the sugars. Cut the cream cheese into 48 small squares.

3. In a small microwaveable bowl, melt the butter.

4. Remove the rolls from the tube and separate them, then cut each roll into 6 wedges. Use your fingers to stretch each piece into an approximately 2-inch square. Place one piece of cream cheese in the center of each piece of dough and bring the dough edges around it, pinching to seal tightly. Working in batches, drop the dough balls into the bowl of butter and turn to coat. Then drop the dough balls into the bag of sugar and shake to coat. As you work, place each coated ball in the slow cooker, seam-side down.

5. Sprinkle the sugar remaining in the bag over the top, followed by the butter remaining in the bowl. Cover and cook on Low for 2 to 2½ hours. When the center pieces are firm and the edges just begin to look crispy, remove the insert from the slow cooker and set it on a wire rack for at least 10 minutes. Carefully remove the "bites" from the slow cooker by using the parchment paper to lift them out in one piece and invert onto a serving platter. Let cool slightly before serving.

3

Classic Recipes

It's fun to experiment with new and unusual recipes, but sometimes there's nothing better than sticking with tried-and-true classics. The kind that your parents used to make for dinner every night. They're sentimental recipes that bring back nostalgic memories, and no recipe collection is complete without them.

Beef Stroganoff

Yield: Serves 4 to 6 | Prep Time: 35 minutes | Cook Time: 6 hours

This traditional Russian dish dates back to the mid-nineteenth century and has been tweaked, refined, and perfected to become the dish we know and love today. It was popularized in America in the 1950s and has been a staple ever since.

INGREDIENTS

2 tablespoons all-purpose flour

1 teaspoon sweet paprika

½ teaspoon kosher salt

¼ teaspoon freshly ground black pepper

1½ pounds beef round or chuck roast, trimmed and cut into 1½-inch cubes

2 tablespoons olive oil

12 ounces white mushrooms, halved

1 cup coarsely chopped onion

1 (14-ounce) can beef broth

1 tablespoon tomato paste

2 sprigs fresh thyme, or ½ teaspoon dried thyme, plus fresh thyme sprigs for garnish

¾ cup sour cream

2 teaspoons Dijon mustard

8 ounces wide egg noodles, cooked and drained

DIRECTIONS

1. Spray the insert of a 6-quart slow cooker with cooking spray.

2. In a large zip-top plastic bag or large bowl, whisk together the flour, sweet paprika, salt, and pepper. Add the beef and toss well to coat with all the seasoned flour.

3. In a large nonstick skillet, heat 1 tablespoon of the olive oil over medium-high heat. Working in two batches, add the beef and cook until well browned on all sides, about 5 minutes per batch. As you finish each batch, transfer the beef to the slow cooker.

4. In the same skillet, heat the remaining 1 tablespoon olive oil. Add the mushrooms and onion and cook, tossing frequently, until the mushrooms exude their juices and begin to brown, about 5 minutes. Add the broth, tomato paste, and thyme and bring to a boil, 5 to 8 minutes. Transfer the mixture to the slow cooker.

5. Cover and cook on Low for 6 hours.

6. In a small bowl, mix together the sour cream and mustard. Add to the stew and stir to incorporate. Turn the slow cooker off but replace the cover and let stand for 10 minutes.

7. Serve the stew over the egg noodles, garnished with thyme sprigs.

Chicken Parmesan

Yield: Serves 4 | Prep Time: 15 minutes | Cook Time: 4 hours

You can't deny the charm of Italian American recipes, and who doesn't love chicken Parm! This one's a favorite to make and eat in my house, and the secret lies in the three different types of prepared tomatoes we use. They add a flavorful kick that complements the melted cheese and moist chicken perfectly.

INGREDIENTS

4 small (4–6-ounce) or 2 large (8-ounce) boneless, skinless chicken breasts

1 (28-ounce) can fire-roasted diced tomatoes, with their juices

1 (8-ounce) can tomato sauce

¼ cup tomato paste

3 garlic cloves, minced

2 tablespoons chopped fresh basil leaves, plus fresh basil sprigs for garnish

4 ounces mozzarella cheese, cut into 4 slices

Kosher salt

1 (16-ounce) box spaghetti

1 tablespoon olive oil

¼ cup panko bread crumbs

¼ cup grated Parmesan cheese

DIRECTIONS

1. Spray the insert of a 6-quart slow cooker with cooking spray.

2. If using large chicken breasts, cut the breasts in half horizontally and open them like a book to make them about ½ inch thick, then cut each into two equal pieces.

3. In a medium bowl, combine the fire-roasted tomatoes, tomato sauce, tomato paste, garlic, and basil. Stir to mix well, then pour into the slow cooker. Lay the chicken pieces on top, cover the slow cooker, and cook on High for 4 hours.

4. About 20 minutes before the chicken has finished cooking, bring a large pot of salted water to a boil.

5. Turn off the slow cooker, uncover, and lay a slice of mozzarella on each piece of chicken. Replace the lid and let sit for 10 minutes, until the cheese has melted.

6. Add the spaghetti to the boiling water and cook according to the package directions until al dente. Drain and set aside.

7. Meanwhile, in a small skillet, heat the olive oil over medium heat. Add the panko and toast until golden brown.

8. Serve the chicken over the cooked spaghetti. Sprinkle the bread crumbs over each piece of chicken and add a dusting of Parmesan. Garnish with basil sprigs.

Chili

Yield: Serves 6 | Prep Time: 20 minutes | Cook Time: 6 to 7 hours on Low or 4 hours on High

It's not quite fall until you break out the chili. It was my traditional dinner on Halloween when I was a kid. I'd go out trick-or-treating with friends for a few hours, then stop back at my house for a bowl of chili. Once I was revitalized, I'd head out for a second pass at the other side of the neighborhood. I can't imagine fall without this chili.

INGREDIENTS

1 pound ground beef

1 green bell pepper, chopped

1 onion, chopped

2 garlic cloves, minced

1 (15-ounce) can dark kidney beans, drained

1 (15-ounce) can pinto beans, drained

2 (14.5-ounce) cans fire-roasted diced tomatoes

1 tablespoon chili powder

1 teaspoon ground cumin

¼ teaspoon cayenne pepper

1 teaspoon kosher salt

½ teaspoon freshly ground black pepper

Grated cheddar cheese, for serving

Sour cream, for serving

Chopped scallions, for serving

DIRECTIONS

1. Lightly spray the insert of a 6-quart slow cooker with cooking spray.

2. In a large skillet, brown the ground beef over medium heat for about 10 minutes, then drain the grease from the skillet.

3. Add the bell pepper, onion, and garlic and cook for 3 to 5 minutes more until the vegetables are softened.

4. Add the ground beef mixture to the slow cooker.

5. Add the kidney beans, pinto beans, fire-roasted tomatoes, chili powder, cumin, cayenne, salt, and black pepper to the slow cooker. Mix to combine.

6. Cook on Low for 6 to 7 hours or on High for 4 hours.

7. Serve garnished with cheese, sour cream, and scallions.

Buffalo Chicken Sandwiches

Yield: Serves 8 | Prep Time: 15 minutes | Cook Time: 6 hours on Low or 4 hours on High

Buffalo chicken has become a signature flavor of mine. I made a different buffalo chicken recipe on television last summer while competing on *Food Network Star*! Whenever I host a backyard barbecue, there's a station for pulled meat with a stack of buns nearby. Pulled chicken is easy to cook in bulk, and the slow cooker keeps the meat warm as everyone moseys through at their leisure.

INGREDIENTS

2 pounds boneless, skinless chicken breasts or thighs, or a combination

½ cup chopped onion

½ cup buffalo sauce, plus more as needed

2 tablespoons dry ranch dressing mix

1 tablespoon honey

1 tablespoon unsalted butter, softened

24 slider-size buns, or 12 regular hamburger buns, toasted

Blue cheese dressing, for serving

Celery sticks, for serving

DIRECTIONS

1. Spray the insert of a 6-quart slow cooker with cooking spray.

2. Arrange the chicken over the bottom of the slow cooker and top with the onion.

3. In a small bowl, combine the buffalo sauce, ranch dressing mix, honey, and butter and stir until well mixed, then pour over the chicken and onion. Cover and cook on Low for 6 hours or on High for 4 hours.

4. Use a slotted spoon to remove the chicken from the slow cooker and shred the meat with two forks. Return the shredded chicken to the slow cooker, toss, and taste, then add up to ½ cup of additional buffalo sauce and toss well. Keep the chicken in the slow cooker on Warm until ready to serve.

5. Assemble the sliders by spooning some of the shredded chicken onto the bottom half of each bun. Drizzle with blue cheese dressing, top with the top half of each bun, and serve with celery sticks on the side.

Corned Beef and Cabbage

Yield: Serves 6 | Prep Time: 15 minutes | Cook Time: 8 to 10 hours on Low or 4 to 5 hours on High

Corned Beef and Cabbage might be one of the most traditional Irish dishes, and you don't have to wait for St. Patrick's Day to make it. It's a warm and cozy favorite that's unexpected and delicious all year long. It's also a fun meal to serve for friends.

INGREDIENTS

1 head purple cabbage

1 large onion, quartered

1 (3–4 pound) corned beef brisket

1 corned beef seasoning packet

Thyme sprigs, for garnish

DIRECTIONS

1. Lightly spray the insert of a 6-quart slow cooker with cooking spray.

2. Place the cabbage and onion in the bottom of the slow cooker.

3. Place the corned beef brisket fat-side up over the cabbage. Sprinkle the seasoning packet over the corned beef. Pour 1½ cups water around the cabbage and corned beef.

4. Cover and cook on Low for 8 to 10 hours or on High for 4 to 5 hours, until the corned beef is tender and the cabbage is cooked.

5. Serve, garnished with thyme.

NOTES

This dish is also good with Yukon Gold potatoes, cut into 1-inch pieces.

4-Cheese Vegetarian Eggplant Parmesan

Yield: Serves 6 to 8 | **Prep Time: 45 minutes** | **Cook Time: 8 hours on Low or 4 hours on High**

Fancied-up vegetables are a great way to appeal to your friends and family when they're trying to eat healthier. (Check out our Gluten-Free Zucchini Bread on page 208 for another favorite.) We use four different kinds of cheese to add four levels of awesome to this classic dish, and this is one I teach children when talking about healthy eating.

INGREDIENTS

4 pounds eggplant, peeled and cut into ⅓-inch-thick rounds

1 tablespoon kosher salt

3 large eggs

½ cup whole milk

1½ cups dry bread crumbs

3 ounces shredded Parmesan cheese

2 teaspoons Italian seasoning

¼ teaspoon red pepper flakes

5 cups prepared marinara sauce

8 ounces part-skim ricotta cheese

12 ounces mozzarella cheese, shredded

4 ounces sliced provolone cheese

Fresh thyme, for garnish

DIRECTIONS

1. Line a baking sheet with paper towels and place the eggplant slices on top. Sprinkle the salt over the eggplant and let sit for 30 minutes. Rinse the salt off the eggplant and pat dry.

2. In a shallow dish or pie plate, whisk together the eggs and milk. In another shallow dish or pie plate, combine the bread crumbs, Parmesan, Italian seasoning, and red pepper flakes.

3. Spray the insert of a 6-quart slow cooker with cooking spray. Spread 2 cups of the marinara sauce over the bottom of the slow cooker.

4. Dip the eggplant into the egg mixture, letting any excess drip off, then into the bread crumb mixture, pressing to coat.

5. Layer one-third of the eggplant over the sauce. Top with 1 cup of the remaining marinara sauce and dollop with ⅓ of the ricotta. Sprinkle with ⅓ of the mozzarella and layer with ⅓ of the provolone. Repeat these layers twice more.

6. Cover and cook on Low for 8 hours or on High for 4 hours.

7. Garnish with fresh thyme and serve.

From-Scratch Italian Lasagna

Yield: Serves 6 | Prep Time: 45 minutes | Cook Time: 4 to 5 hours on Low or 2 to 2½ hours on High

Lasagna is the ultimate comfort food and a perfect dish if your family members are eating dinner at different times. I can eat a slice at five and my husband can dig in around seven when he's home from work. Each forkful is filled with layers upon layers of cheesy, saucy, noodle-y goodness that is impossible to resist. This particular recipe is unique because it uses both ground beef and Italian sausage for double the flavor!

INGREDIENTS

2 tablespoons olive oil

½ pound ground beef

1 pound bulk Italian sausage

1 large onion, chopped

½ teaspoon kosher salt

½ teaspoon freshly ground black pepper

¼ teaspoon red pepper flakes

1 teaspoon Italian seasoning

2 tablespoon chopped fresh parsley

2 teaspoons garlic powder

2 tablespoons Worcestershire sauce

1 (6-ounce) can tomato paste

1 (29-ounce) can tomato sauce

2 tablespoons sugar

4 cups shredded mozzarella cheese

1½ cups part-skim ricotta cheese

½ cup grated Parmesan cheese

8 ounces regular (not no-boil) lasagna noodles, uncooked

Shredded Parmesan cheese, for garnish

DIRECTIONS

1. Spray the insert of a 6-quart slow cooker with cooking spray.

2. In a large skillet, heat the olive oil over medium heat. Add the ground beef, sausage, and onion. Cook until the beef has browned, about 10 minutes. Add the salt, black pepper, red pepper flakes, Italian seasoning, parsley, garlic powder, Worcestershire sauce, tomato paste, tomato sauce, sugar, and 1¼ cups water. Stir well and simmer for 20 minutes.

3. In a large bowl, combine the mozzarella, ricotta, and grated Parmesan.

4. Spread one-quarter of the meat sauce over the bottom of the slow cooker. Arrange one-third of the noodles over the sauce, breaking the noodles to fit if necessary.

5. Spoon one-third of the cheese mixture over the noodles and spread it evenly.

6. Repeat the layers twice.

7. Top with the remaining meat sauce.

8. Cover and cook on Low for 4 to 5 hours or on High for 2 to 2½ hours.

9. Garnish with shredded Parmesan. Cut into squares and serve.

Ritz Cracker Meat Loaf

Yield: Serves 8 | Prep Time: 15 minutes | Cook Time: 6 to 8 hours on Low or 3 to 4 hours on High

Ritz crackers add so much flavor to this meat loaf. Their buttery, salty texture helps keep the meat loaf nice and moist, while the green peppers add color. This is a fun way to twist the classic, and your kids will love snacking on the leftover crackers.

INGREDIENTS

2 pounds lean ground beef

½ cup chopped green bell pepper

½ cup chopped onion

2 large eggs

1½ teaspoons kosher salt

1 cup Ritz cracker crumbs (about 24 crackers)

1½ cups ketchup

1 teaspoon yellow mustard

¼ cup packed light brown sugar

Fresh thyme, for garnish

DIRECTIONS

1. Line the insert of a 6-quart slow cooker with aluminum foil and spray with cooking spray.

2. In a medium bowl, combine the ground beef, bell pepper, onion, eggs, salt, cracker crumbs, and ¾ cup of the ketchup. Use a spoon or your hands to mix until the ingredients are incorporated.

3. Shape the meat mixture into a loaf and place it in the slow cooker.

4. Cook on Low for 6 to 8 hours or on High for 3 to 4 hours, until the meat is no longer pink.

5. In the last 15 minutes of cooking, in a small bowl, mix together the remaining ketchup, mustard, and brown sugar and spread on top of the meat loaf. Cook for the remaining 15 minutes.

6. Let cool. Slice and serve with fresh thyme.

Chicken Cordon Bleu

Yield: Serves 6 | Prep Time: 15 minutes | Cook Time: 4 to 6 hours on Low or 2 to 3 hours on High

This elegant French dinner is an impressive dish to serve up when you're looking to make something fancy-schmancy. I whipped it up once for some business associates, and they were raving about it all night long! The stuffing on top gives it a cozy nostalgia, like a holiday meal, spreading warm feelings all around.

INGREDIENTS

1 (10.75-ounce) can cream of chicken soup

1 cup half-and-half

1 tablespoon Dijon mustard

5–6 boneless, skinless chicken breasts

4 ounces sliced ham

4 ounces sliced Jarlsberg cheese

6 ounces herbed stuffing mix

4 tablespoons (½ stick) unsalted butter, melted

¼ cup chicken broth

DIRECTIONS

1. Lightly spray the insert of a 6-quart slow cooker with cooking spray.

2. In a medium bowl, combine the cream of chicken soup, half-and-half, and mustard. Pour half the mixture over the bottom of the slow cooker.

3. Layer the chicken over the chicken soup mixture.

4. Layer the ham and then the cheese over the chicken.

5. Pour the remaining soup mixture evenly over the top, then sprinkle the herb stuffing evenly over the soup mixture.

6. Drizzle the melted butter and then the broth on top.

7. Cook on Low for 4 to 6 hours or on High for 2 to 3 hours. Serve.

Melt-in-Your-Mouth Pot Roast

Yield: Serves 4 to 6 | Prep Time: 20 minutes | Cook Time: 5 to 6 hours

The ideal pot roast is one that falls apart in your mouth. This slow cooker version really does the trick, serving up wholesome veggies and juicy, tender meat in each bite.

INGREDIENTS

1½ pounds russet potatoes, unpeeled, cut into 1½-inch chunks

1 pound baby carrots

1 cup coarsely chopped onion

6–8 boneless, skinless chicken thighs

4 tablespoons (½ stick) unsalted butter

½ cup finely chopped onion

½ cup finely chopped celery

2 tablespoons chopped fresh parsley, plus more for garnish

¼ cup all-purpose flour

½ teaspoon kosher salt

½ teaspoon freshly ground black pepper

1 cup chicken broth

DIRECTIONS

1. Spray the insert of a 6-quart slow cooker with cooking spray.

2. Layer the potatoes, carrots, and coarsely chopped onion over the bottom of the slow cooker and place the chicken thighs on top.

3. In a small saucepan, melt the butter over medium heat. Add the finely chopped onion, celery, and parsley and cook until the vegetables are translucent, about 2 minutes. Add the flour, stirring until the flour is completely absorbed, about 1 minute. Add the salt, pepper, and chicken broth and cook, stirring, until the sauce thickens and bubbles, about 2 minutes. Pour the sauce over the chicken, cover, and cook on Low for 5 to 6 hours, or until the vegetables appear done when pierced with the tip of a knife.

4. Serve, garnished with parsley.

Pulled Pork

Yield: Serves 8 | Prep Time: 10 minutes | Cook Time: 6 hours

This Southern barbecue specialty is a staple all year long when you use your slow cooker! I like serving Pulled Pork alongside fresh coleslaw and potato wedges or on buns with sliced red onions.

INGREDIENTS

1 (4-pound) boneless pork shoulder

1 (28-ounce) bottle barbecue sauce

¼ cup sriracha

¼ cup honey

1 teaspoon kosher salt

1 teaspoon freshly ground black pepper

1 tablespoon chili powder

Multigrain buns, your choice, for serving

Red cabbage slaw, for serving

Sliced scallions, for serving

DIRECTIONS

1. Spray the insert of a 6-quart slow cooker with cooking spray.

2. Place the pork shoulder in the slow cooker.

3. In a medium bowl, combine the barbecue sauce, sriracha, honey, salt, pepper, and chili powder. Pour into the slow cooker over the meat.

4. Cook on Low for 6 hours. Remove the pork shoulder from the slow cooker and use two forks to shred the meat; discard any large pieces of fat. Return the meat to the slow cooker and stir to coat with the sauce.

5. Serve the pork on multigrain buns, topped with red cabbage slaw and scallions.

NOTE

To make red cabbage slaw, whisk together ½ cup apple cider vinegar and 2 tablespoons sugar in a large bowl until sugar dissolves. Slowly whisk in ¼ cup extra virgin olive oil, 2 teaspoons celery seed, and salt and pepper to taste. Toss in ½ head of thinly sliced red cabbage and 1 small red onion, diced. Cover and let set for at least 1 hour.

Sweet Sesame Ribs

Yield: Serves 4 to 6 | Prep Time: 5 minutes plus 2 hours marinating time | Cook Time: 6 hours

I hope you have some wet wipes handy, because you won't be able to resist diving right into this sticky mess. This recipe uses a few different kinds of sauces for a sweet kick that'll make these ribs stand out from all the rest.

INGREDIENTS

2 large oranges

½ cup soy sauce

½ cup hoisin sauce

¼ cup honey

¼ cup bottled sweet chili sauce

3 tablespoons rice vinegar

2 tablespoons toasted sesame oil

1 tablespoon minced fresh garlic

4–5 pounds baby back ribs, ends of ribs trimmed

2 tablespoons cornstarch

DIRECTIONS

1. Zest and juice 1 of the oranges. Place the zest and juice in a large zip-top plastic bag and add the soy sauce, hoisin sauce, honey, sweet chili sauce, vinegar, sesame oil, and garlic. Mix well and add the baby back ribs. Close the bag and shake to coat the ribs completely. Marinate in the refrigerator for at least 2 hours or up to overnight.

2. Spray the insert of a 6-quart slow cooker with cooking spray.

3. Transfer the ribs and marinade from the bag into the slow cooker. Cover and cook on Low for 6 hours.

4. Transfer the ribs to a warm platter and put the juices in a small saucepan over medium heat.

5. In a small bowl, combine the cornstarch and 2 tablespoons water to make a smooth paste. Stir the cornstarch slurry into the pot with the juices from the ribs and cook, stirring occasionally, until the sauce thickens.

6. Cut the ribs into chunks and toss with the sauce. Zest and slice the remaining orange. Garnish with the orange zest and serve with the orange slices on the side.

Roasted Chicken

Yield: Serves 4 to 6 | Prep Time: 20 minutes | Cook Time: 4 to 4½ hours

Not only can you enjoy Roasted Chicken for dinner, but you'll wind up with plenty of leftovers you can throw into a soup, add to the top of a salad, or turn into a sandwich. By making this in the slow cooker, you'll free up oven space for your favorite sides or a pie for dessert.

INGREDIENTS

1 whole chicken (about 5 pounds)

1 lemon, halved

1 garlic head, halved crosswise

3–4 sprigs fresh rosemary

1 teaspoon kosher salt

1 teaspoon freshly ground black pepper

1 tablespoon paprika

1 teaspoon herbes de Provence

¼ teaspoon cayenne pepper

1 large onion, chopped

Fresh herbs, such as thyme and rosemary, for garnish

DIRECTIONS

1. Lightly spray the insert of a 6-quart slow cooker with cooking spray.

2. Discard the giblets, if they were included with your chicken. Rinse the chicken and pat dry.

3. Place the lemon, garlic, and rosemary inside the cavity of the chicken.

4. Season the inside and outside of the chicken with the salt and black pepper.

5. In a small bowl, mix the paprika, herbes de Provence, and cayenne. Rub the seasoning mixture over the chicken.

6. Spread the chopped onion over the bottom of the slow cooker. Set the chicken on top, breast-side up.

7. Cover and cook on High for 4 to 4½ hours, until the chicken registers 165°F on an instant-read thermometer.

8. Garnish with fresh herbs and serve.

Smothered Pork Chops in Mushroom Sauce

Yield: Serves 6 | Prep Time: 20 minutes | Cook Time: 3 to 3½ hours

If you're having a rough day and just need a recipe that feels like a hug, then these Smothered Pork Chops are all you need to turn it around. The thick-and-creamy mushroom sauce will warm you up from the inside out.

INGREDIENTS

6 boneless pork chops, ¾-inch thick (about 6 ounces each)

¼ cup all-purpose flour

½ teaspoon steak seasoning

½ teaspoon kosher salt

3 teaspoons olive oil

½ cup sliced onion

8 ounces sliced mushrooms

1 (14.5-ounce) can beef or chicken broth

Fresh thyme, for garnish

DIRECTIONS

1. Spray the insert of a 6-quart slow cooker with cooking spray.

2. Place the pork chops in a large zip-top plastic bag and add the flour, steak seasoning, and salt. Close the bag and shake to coat the pork chops completely.

3. In a large nonstick skillet, heat 1½ teaspoons of the olive oil over medium-high heat. Remove the pork chops from the zip-top bag and brown in the skillet until golden brown, about 3 minutes per side. Reserve the bag of seasoned flour.

4. Transfer the pork chops to the slow cooker and arrange them in one layer over the bottom. In the same skillet, cook the onion over medium-high heat, stirring, for 2 minutes, until translucent. Add the remaining 1½ teaspoons olive oil and the mushrooms and cook, stirring, for 2 minutes more, until the mushrooms begin to brown. Sprinkle the onion and mushrooms with the reserved flour mixture and cook until the flour has been absorbed, about 1 minute. Add the broth and cook, stirring, until the mixture comes to a boil and begins to thicken, 3 to 5 minutes.

5. Pour the mixture into the slow cooker over the pork chops, cover, and cook on Low for 3 to 3½ hours, depending on the thickness of the pork chops.

6. Serve, garnished with fresh thyme.

Stuffed Peppers

Yield: Serves 6 | Prep Time: 20 minutes | Cook Time: 4 to 5 hours on Low or 2 to 3 hours on High

I love to make a batch of these to store in my freezer for a few weeks until I'm ready to reheat for a quick, ready-made dinner. What's not to love? You have veggies and protein all wrapped up in a neat, tidy package. It's exactly what I need at the end of a busy day.

INGREDIENTS

6 bell peppers

1 pound lean ground turkey

1½ cups cooked rice (brown or white)

1½ cups shredded cheddar cheese

1 (15-ounce) can black beans, drained and rinsed

1 cup frozen corn

1 (12-ounce) can Ro-Tel tomatoes

3 tablespoons chopped fresh cilantro

2 teaspoons ground cumin

½ teaspoon chili powder, or more to taste

Kosher salt and freshly ground black pepper

Sour cream, for serving

Guacamole, for serving

DIRECTIONS

1. Lightly spray the insert of a 6-quart slow cooker with cooking spray.

2. Cut the tops off the bell peppers and scrape out the seeds and ribs.

3. In a large bowl, combine the turkey, rice, 1 cup of the cheese, the black beans, corn, tomatoes, cilantro, cumin, chili powder, and salt and black pepper to taste. Spoon the filling into each hollowed-out bell pepper.

4. Place the peppers upright in the slow cooker, leaning the peppers against one another as necessary. Cover and cook on Low for 4 to 5 hours or on High for 2 to 3 hours. The stuffed peppers are ready when the outsides are tender and the turkey is no longer pink.

5. Top the peppers with the remaining ½ cup of cheese. Cover and cook on Low until the cheese has melted, about 10 minutes.

6. Serve immediately, with sour cream and guacamole alongside.

Lemon Pepper Chicken Breasts

Yield: Serves 5 | Prep Time: 15 minutes | Cook Time: 3 to 4 hours

Lemon Pepper Chicken is one of those weeknight dinners that's easy to pull out at a moment's notice. It uses pantry-staple ingredients and has such a quick prep time, but the classic lemon pepper flavor combo still makes this a winner.

INGREDIENTS

½ cup all-purpose flour

1 teaspoon freshly ground black pepper, plus more as needed

4 boneless, skinless chicken breasts

4 tablespoons (½ stick) unsalted butter

1 (1-ounce) package Italian dressing mix

½ cup fresh lemon juice

½ cup chicken broth

1 lemon

Kosher salt

Sliced scallions, for garnish

Cooked white rice, for serving

DIRECTIONS

1. Lightly spray the insert of a 6-quart slow cooker with cooking spray.

2. In a shallow dish or pie plate, combine the flour and pepper. Dredge the chicken in the flour mixture, full coating all sides.

3. In a medium skillet, melt the butter over medium heat. Add the chicken. Lightly brown each side to lightly crisp the breading, 3 to 5 minutes. The chicken will not be cooked through but will finish cooking in the slow cooker.

4. Transfer the chicken to the slow cooker. Sprinkle the Italian dressing mix over the top of the chicken.

5. In a small bowl, whisk together the lemon juice and broth. Pour over the chicken and seasonings.

6. Cook on Low for 3 to 4 hours.

7. Zest the lemon and slice the lemon into wheels.

8. Before serving, sprinkle with the lemon zest, salt, pepper, and scallions. Serve with the lemon wheels and cooked rice.

Tuna Casserole

Yield: Serves 4 | Prep Time: 10 minutes | Cook Time: 6 hours on Low or 2 hours on High

I love tuna salad. Tuna Casserole. Tuna anything! The creaminess of the mushroom soup mixed with the soft egg noodles and crunchy onion creates an array of textures that makes this tuna casserole memorable.

INGREDIENTS

2¾ cups dry egg noodles

1 teaspoon kosher salt

½ teaspoon freshly ground black pepper

½ cup chopped onion

1 (6.5-ounce) can tuna

1 cup frozen peas

1 (10.75-ounce) can cream of mushroom soup

½ (10.75-ounce) can chicken broth

½ cup shredded white cheddar cheese

½ cup panko bread crumbs

1 tablespoon unsalted butter, melted

1 teaspoon herbes de Provence

Sliced scallions, for garnish

DIRECTIONS

1. Lightly spray the insert of a 6-quart slow cooker with cooking spray.

2. Place the noodles in the bottom of the slow cooker. Top with the salt, pepper, onion, tuna, peas, cream of mushroom soup, and broth. Stir.

3. Top evenly with the cheese.

4. In a small bowl, combine the panko, melted butter, and herbes de Provence. Sprinkle the seasoned panko evenly over the tuna mixture.

5. Cover and cook on Low for 6 hours or on High for 2 hours.

6. Ladle onto plates, garnish with scallions, and serve.

4

Dinner Recipes

Dinnertime is everyone's chance to unwind for the day. You settle in with your family and discuss everything that went on, enjoying your food as you go. Slow cooker recipes allow you to relax after a long day of work and errands, comforted by the knowledge that a home-cooked meal is ready and waiting when dinnertime rolls around.

Baked Ziti

Yield: Serves 8 | Prep Time: 25 minutes | Cook Time: 5 hours on Low or 3 hours on High

Pasta nights are some of our favorite nights in my house. I love playing around with different shapes and throwing in new cheeses and spices to suit my mood. I used rigatoni pasta for this recipe, but if you'd like to try out a different shape, go for it.

INGREDIENTS

5 cups fresh spinach leaves

½ cup fresh basil leaves

15 ounces ricotta cheese

1 large egg

¾ cup grated Parmesan cheese

1½ cups Italian four-cheese mix

½ teaspoon kosher salt

1 pound rigatoni pasta, uncooked

48 ounces basil-flavored pasta sauce

Fresh basil, for garnish

DIRECTIONS

1. Spray the insert of a 6-quart slow cooker with cooking spray.

2. Wash the spinach and basil and shake to dry, leaving some water on the leaves. Place them in a large microwaveable bowl, cover with microwave-safe plastic wrap, and microwave for 2 minutes. Dry well between paper towels and coarsely chop.

3. In a medium bowl, combine the ricotta, egg, ½ cup of the Parmesan, ½ cup of the four-cheese mix, the salt, and the chopped spinach and basil.

4. Place 3 cups of the rigatoni in the bottom of the prepared slow cooker. Top with 2 cups of the pasta sauce and spread the sauce to be sure all the noodles are submerged and coated with the sauce. Top with half the ricotta mixture. Layer on the remaining noodles, 2 cups of the pasta sauce, the remaining ricotta, and finally the remaining pasta sauce. Spread the final layer of pasta sauce evenly to submerge all the pasta.

5. Place three long pieces of paper towel over the top of the slow cooker and cover with the lid.

6. Cook on Low for 5 hours or on High for 3 hours. Check to see if the pasta is cooked before turning off the slow cooker; if the pasta is still too firm, cook for 20 minutes more.

7. Remove the lid of the slow cooker and sprinkle the remaining four-cheese mix over the top, then the remaining Parmesan. Cover and let the pasta stand for 10 minutes more to melt the cheese.

8. Serve warm, garnished with fresh basil.

French Dip Sandwiches

Yield: 6 sandwiches | Prep Time: 15 minutes | Cook Time: 6 to 8 hours

The contrast of the crusty French bread and the tender, juicy meat brings this sandwich to the next level. By making it in the slow cooker, you can prep the dish in the morning, run your errands, and have a home-cooked lunch waiting for you at home.

INGREDIENTS

2 pounds chuck roast

2 tablespoons olive oil

½ teaspoon kosher salt

¼ teaspoon freshly ground black pepper

1 cup sliced onion

1 (14.5-ounce) can beef broth

1 tablespoon Worcestershire sauce

1 bay leaf

12 (6-inch) Italian-style rolls, or French baguettes, halved and cut into 6-inch pieces

DIRECTIONS

1. Spray the insert of a 7-quart slow cooker with cooking spray.

2. Rub all surfaces of the chuck roast with 1 tablespoon of the olive oil, the salt, and the pepper.

3. In a large nonstick skillet, heat the remaining 1 tablespoon of the olive oil over medium-high heat. Add the roast and sear all sides until browned, 3 to 5 minutes.

4. While the meat is browning, place the sliced onion in the slow cooker in one layer.

5. Transfer the roast to the slow cooker and pour the broth and Worcestershire sauce over. Add the bay leaf, cover, and cook on Low for 6 to 8 hours.

6. Transfer the meat to a cutting board to cool for 10 minutes. Skim any excess fat from the juices in the slow cooker. Slice the meat into very thin slices and return it to the juices in the slow cooker on the Warm setting until serving time.

7. Preheat the broiler. Place the rolls, cut-side down, to toast for 2 minutes. Place slices of the roast on the bottom halves of the rolls and use a slotted spoon to add some onion slices. Serve with the sauce on the side for dipping.

Sweet Pineapple Ham

Yield: Serves 10 to 12 | Prep Time: 15 minutes | Cook Time: 4 hours on Low or 2 hours on High

The brown sugar and maple syrup glaze turn the ham into a sweet-and-savory treat for dinner. Serve with asparagus, creamy rice, or risotto for a complete meal.

INGREDIENTS

4–5 pounds cooked ham

2–3 whole garlic cloves

½ cup canned crushed pineapple, partially drained

½ cup packed light brown sugar

¼ cup maple syrup

¼ cup country-style Dijon mustard with seeds

DIRECTIONS

1. Spray the insert of a 6-quart slow cooker with cooking spray.

2. Cut through the top surface of the ham in a diamond pattern ½ inch deep, making the diamonds around ½ inch wide. Insert a whole clove into a couple of the diamonds.

3. Place the ham in the slow cooker.

4. In a medium bowl, combine the pineapple, brown sugar, maple syrup, and mustard, stirring to mix well. Brush the ham on all exposed surfaces with half the sauce. Cover and cook on Low for 2 hours or on High for 1 hour.

5. Brush all exposed surfaces with the sauce again and cook on Low for 2 hours more or on High for 1 hour more.

6. Slice the ham and serve with any extra sauce.

Ham and Cheese Potatoes

Yield: Serves 8 | Prep Time: 10 minutes | Cook Time: 4 to 5 hours

The unique factor in this recipe is the addition of Muenster cheese, which provides a sweet, nutty flavor. When the Muenster is combined with the cream, you get a smooth, cheesy, irresistible dish.

INGREDIENTS

1½ pounds sweet potatoes, thinly sliced

1½ pounds russet potatoes, thinly sliced

½ cup all-purpose flour

1 tablespoon minced garlic

1 teaspoon kosher salt

½ teaspoon freshly ground black pepper

8 ounces cooked ham, shredded

4 ounces shredded cheddar cheese

1 cup heavy cream or half-and-half

4 slices Muenster cheese

Fresh thyme, for garnish

DIRECTIONS

1. Spray the insert of a 6-quart slow cooker with cooking spray.

2. In a large bowl, combine the sweet potatoes, russet potatoes, flour, garlic, salt, and pepper and toss to coat.

3. Place half the potatoes in a layer over the bottom of the slow cooker. Top with half the ham and half the cheddar cheese. Add another layer of potatoes, ham, and the remaining cheddar cheese. Pour the cream over the top and arrange the Muenster cheese as a final layer.

4. Cover and cook on Low for 4 to 5 hours. Check after 4 hours to determine if the potatoes are tender; if not, cook for 30 minutes to 1 hour more. Serve immediately or keep warm for up to 2 hours in the slow cooker on the Warm setting. Garnish with fresh thyme and additional salt and pepper, to taste.

Jambalaya

Yield: Serves 4 | Prep Time: 25 minutes | Cook Time: 5 hours

Jambalaya gets its origins from French and Spanish cuisines, creating an unforgettable mash-up. It was sometimes made in big cast-iron pots outdoors to feed large groups of people for weddings or family reunions. This version works well if you're feeding a smaller group.

INGREDIENTS

2 tablespoons vegetable oil

1 cup finely chopped onion

¾ cup finely chopped celery

¾ cup finely chopped red bell pepper

1 tablespoon minced garlic

½ teaspoon dried thyme

½ teaspoon ground oregano

½ teaspoon sweet paprika

½ teaspoon kosher salt

½ teaspoon cayenne pepper

1 small bay leaf

1 pound boneless, skinless chicken thighs, chopped into ½-inch pieces

8 ounces andouille or hot Italian sausage, chopped into ½-inch pieces

1 (14-ounce) can diced tomatoes, with their juices

1 (15-ounce) can chicken broth

¼ cup tomato paste

1 tablespoon Worcestershire sauce

1½ cups brown or converted rice (see Note)

8 ounces peeled and deveined raw shrimp

Fresh parsley, for garnish

DIRECTIONS

1. In a very wide, deep skillet, heat 1 tablespoon of the vegetable oil over medium-high heat. Add the onion, celery, and bell pepper and cook, stirring frequently, until the vegetables are softened, about 3 minutes.

2. Add the garlic, thyme, oregano, paprika, salt, cayenne, and bay leaf and cook, stirring continuously, for 1 minute.

3. Push the vegetables to the edges of the pan and add the remaining 1 tablespoon vegetable oil. Add the chicken thighs and cook, stirring frequently, until browned, about 2 minutes.

4. Add the andouille sausage and cook, stirring, for 2 minutes.

5. Add the tomatoes, broth, tomato paste, Worcestershire sauce, and 1 cup water and stir until the liquids bubble.

6. Pour the mixture into the slow cooker and stir in the rice. Cook on Low for 4½ hours. Taste to see if the rice is nearly tender and adjust the seasonings as necessary.

7. Add the shrimp, remove the bay leaf, and stir well. Cover and cook on Low for 30 minutes more.

8. Serve, garnished with parsley.

NOTES

Brown or converted white rice works best, as regular long-grain rice will get too soft and sticky after long cooking.

Potato Puff Casserole

Yield: Serves 8 | Prep Time: 15 minutes | Cook Time: 4 hours on Low or 2 hours on High

I've seen people at potlucks go crazy for this Potato Puff Casserole. Potato puffs are a crowd favorite no matter how they appear, but when baked into this casserole, their crispy-creamy goodness is impossible to resist.

INGREDIENTS

1 tablespoon vegetable oil

1 pound ground turkey or beef

¾ cup finely chopped onion

1 teaspoon finely minced garlic

6 large eggs

¼ cup sour cream

½ teaspoon red pepper flakes (optional)

½ teaspoon kosher salt

¼ teaspoon freshly ground black pepper

1 (28-ounce) bag frozen potato puffs, regular or mini

1 cup shredded sharp cheddar cheese

2 tablespoons chopped fresh parsley

DIRECTIONS

1. Spray the insert of a 6-quart slow cooker with cooking spray.

2. In a large nonstick skillet, heat the vegetable oil over medium-high heat. Add the turkey and onion and cook, stirring frequently, until the meat begins to brown, 3 minutes. Add the garlic and cook, stirring, for 1 to 2 minutes more. Let cool a few minutes.

3. In a large bowl, whisk together the eggs, sour cream, red pepper flakes (if using), salt, and black pepper.

4. Arrange half the potato puffs in a single layer over the bottom of the slow cooker. Spoon the turkey mixture on top, then pour the egg mixture over all. Sprinkle with the cheese. Add the remaining potato puffs in a single layer and sprinkle with the parsley. Cover and cook on Low for 4 hours or on High for 2 hours.

5. Serve.

Caesar Chicken

Yield: Serves 4 | Prep Time: 10 minutes | Cook Time: 7 hours on Low or 3½ hours on High

Salad dressing doesn't need to be reserved for your lunch hour—it works as a secret ingredient in dinner recipes, too! The Caesar in this recipe helps keep the chicken nice and moist, and it's an easy way to pack in the flavor.

INGREDIENTS

4 boneless, skinless chicken breasts

1 teaspoon kosher salt

½ teaspoon freshly ground black pepper

¼ cup chicken broth

1 (12-ounce) bottle creamy Caesar dressing

½ cup shredded Parmesan cheese

4–8 romaine lettuce leaves

1 cup grape tomatoes, halved

8 (1-inch) slices crusty Italian bread, toasted

DIRECTIONS

1. Lightly spray the insert of a 6-quart slow cooker with cooking spray.

2. Place the chicken in the slow cooker. Sprinkle with the salt and pepper and add the broth.

3. Cook for 6 hours on Low or for 3 hours on High. Drain the liquid from the slow cooker.

4. Pour the Caesar dressing over the chicken, then sprinkle the Parmesan on top.

5. Cook on Low for 1 hour or on High for 30 minutes.

6. On each plate, place 1 chicken breast on 1 or 2 romaine leaves, scatter a few grape tomato halves on top, and serve with 2 slices of toast.

Cheesy Chicken and Rice

Yield: Serves 8 | Prep Time: 10 minutes | Cook Time: 6 to 8 hours on Low or 3 to 4 hours on High

Chicken and rice are a classic combination, like peanut butter and jelly or cookies and milk. They just belong together. We've added a few veggies and some cheese, but we all know it's the chicken and rice that are the stars of the show.

INGREDIENTS

4 boneless, skinless chicken breasts

1 large onion, chopped

1 red bell pepper, chopped

1 (10.5-ounce) can cream of celery soup

1 (8-ounce) box yellow rice mix, cooked according to the package directions

1 (15-ounce) can whole-kernel corn, drained

1 cup shredded cheddar cheese

Chopped scallions, for garnish

DIRECTIONS

1. Lightly spray the insert of a 6-quart slow cooker with cooking spray.

2. Place the chicken in the slow cooker. Top with the onion and bell pepper.

3. Spoon the cream of celery soup over all.

4. Cover and cook on Low for 6 to 8 hours or on High for 3 to 4 hours.

5. Add the yellow rice, corn, and cheese and mix well.

6. Garnish with scallions and serve.

Chicken Broccoli Alfredo

Yield: Serves 6 | Prep Time: 15 minutes | Cook Time: 7 hours on Low or 3½ hours on High

When I first became interested in cooking, I would look for easy restaurant-style recipes I could make for dinner, and Chicken Alfredo was on that list. This version combines classic ingredients to make a simple dinner that any cook can tackle.

INGREDIENTS

1 pound boneless, skinless chicken breasts

½ teaspoon kosher salt, plus more as needed

½ teaspoon freshly ground black pepper

2 (15-ounce) jars Alfredo sauce

1 pound broccoli, cut into florets

1 teaspoon minced garlic

¼ teaspoon red pepper flakes

8 ounces rigatoni pasta

2–3 tablespoons shredded Parmesan cheese

DIRECTIONS

1. Lightly spray the insert of a 6-quart slow cooker with cooking spray.

2. Place the chicken in the slow cooker and sprinkle with the salt and pepper.

3. Pour the Alfredo sauce over the chicken.

4. Cover and cook on Low for 6 hours or on High for 3 hours.

5. Add the broccoli, garlic, and red pepper flakes.

6. Cover and cook on Low for 1 hour or on High for 30 minutes.

7. Meanwhile, bring a large pot of salted water to a boil. Add the rigatoni, and cook according to the package directions until al dente. Drain the rigatoni and add to the slow cooker. Mix in.

8. Sprinkle the Parmesan on top and serve.

Philly Cheesesteaks

Yield: Serves 6 | Prep Time: 30 minutes | Cook Time: 6 hours

The first time I visited Philadelphia and bit into a Philly Cheesesteak, I knew I was in heaven. It was so overstuffed that I could barely fit it into my mouth, but it was well worth it. I love having this recipe handy to make my own version at home without having to travel across the country.

INGREDIENTS

2 onions, cut into thick slices

2 green bell peppers, cut into ¼-inch slices

⅓ cup chopped fresh parsley

2 tablespoons Worcestershire sauce

2 teaspoons light brown sugar

2 large garlic cloves, slivered (about 2 tablespoons)

½ teaspoon kosher salt

½ teaspoon freshly ground black pepper

1¾ pounds chuck eye roast, trimmed of any excess fat

8 ounces mushrooms, sliced

3 cups beef broth

8 hoagie rolls, for serving

8 slices provolone cheese, for topping

DIRECTIONS

1. Spray the insert of a 7-quart slow cooker with cooking spray.

2. Arrange the onions and bell peppers over the bottom of the slow cooker.

3. In a large bowl, combine the parsley, Worcestershire sauce, brown sugar, garlic, salt, and black pepper. Add the chuck eye roast and turn to coat well.

4. Place the roast in the slow cooker, add the mushrooms and broth, and pour any remaining Worcestershire sauce mixture on top. Cover and cook on Low for 6 hours.

5. Remove the roast from the slow cooker and let stand for 15 to 20 minutes to cool, then slice very thinly and return the slices to the juices in the slow cooker.

6. Preheat the broiler.

7. Halve each roll horizontally. Spoon the roast slices onto the bottom halves of the rolls and use a slotted spoon to add some onion, bell pepper, and mushrooms on top of the meat. Lay a slice of provolone on each and broil until the cheese has melted, about 4 minutes. Quickly dip the tops of the rolls in the sauce and close each sandwich.

8. Serve immediately.

Pierogi Casserole with Sausage

Yield: Serves 6 | Prep Time: 15 minutes | Cook Time: 3 hours

Store-bought frozen pierogi cut your work in half. With minimal chopping required and a super-quick prep time, you can squeeze making a semi-homemade dinner between errands on the weekend.

INGREDIENTS

24 store-bought frozen potato pierogi (about 28 ounces), slightly thawed

1 pound precooked kielbasa, cut into 2-inch pieces

4 cups chicken broth

1 (8-ounce) package cream cheese, cut into cubes

1 cup shredded cheddar cheese

Chopped fresh parsley, for garnish

DIRECTIONS

1. Spray the insert of a 6-quart slow cooker with cooking spray.

2. Lay half the pierogi in a single layer over the bottom of the slow cooker. Add about half the kielbasa pieces in a single layer.

3. In a medium microwaveable bowl, combine 1 cup of the broth and the cream cheese and microwave on 70% power for 2 minutes. Whisk until completely smooth, then gently whisk in the remaining broth. Pour half the mixture over the pierogi and sausage and top with half the cheddar cheese.

4. With the remaining ingredients, make layers of pierogi, sausage, the cream cheese mixture, and finally the remaining shredded cheese.

5. Cover and cook on High for 3 hours.

6. Garnish with parsley and serve.

Bourbon Chicken

Yield: Serves 6 | Prep Time: 15 minutes | Cook Time: 6 hours on Low or 3 hours on High

Chicken thighs don't get the praise they deserve. They're full of flavor and make a perfect budget-friendly option for dinner. If I am lucky, my husband will share some of his bourbon, and the crushed pineapple in this recipe adds an extra-tart burst of flavor. It's the perfect Sunday dinner.

INGREDIENTS

3 pounds boneless, skinless chicken thighs

¼ cup soy sauce

1 tablespoon chopped fresh ginger

1 tablespoon chopped fresh garlic

½ cup canned crushed pineapple

¼ cup bourbon

3 tablespoons ketchup

3 tablespoons rice vinegar

2 tablespoons light brown sugar

1 tablespoon maple syrup

¼–½ teaspoon red pepper flakes

¼ teaspoon kosher salt

Cooked rice, for serving

Chopped scallions, for garnish

DIRECTIONS

1. Spray the insert of a 6-quart slow cooker with cooking spray.

2. Trim the fat off the chicken as necessary, but leave the pieces whole. Place the chicken in a large zip-top plastic bag and add the soy sauce.

3. In a small bowl, mash the ginger and garlic together into a paste and add to the bag; close and massage the bag with your hands to coat the chicken well. Let stand while preparing the remaining ingredients, or refrigerate for up to 24 hours.

4. In a medium bowl, combine the pineapple, bourbon, ketchup, vinegar, brown sugar, maple syrup, red pepper flakes, and salt and stir to mix. (This may be made ahead of time and refrigerated for up to 24 hours.)

5. Place the chicken in the slow cooker and pour the sauce over the top, stirring to coat the chicken. Cover and cook on Low for 6 hours or on High for 3 hours.

6. Serve over cooked rice, garnished with chopped scallions.

Soba Noodles with Vegetables

Yield: Serves 4 | Prep Time: 20 minutes | Cook Time: 8 hours

This Japanese noodle dish is restaurant-quality good and perfect for impressing company or for a fun and interactive date night for two, but still only takes 20 minutes to prep before letting the slow cooker do all the work.

INGREDIENTS

3 carrots, quartered crosswise

1 onion, quartered

1 cup dried shiitake mushrooms

1 (4-inch) piece fresh ginger, leave whole

2 garlic cloves

2 tablespoons soy sauce

1 (32-ounce) box low-sodium chicken broth

4 boneless chicken thighs

8 ounces soba noodles

1 cup coarsely chopped bok choy

1 (8-ounce) can bamboo shoots

1 (15-ounce) can baby corn

4 scallions, chopped

4 "3-minute" boiled eggs, peeled (see Notes)

Chile oil, for serving (optional)

DIRECTIONS

1. Spray the insert of a 6-quart slow cooker with cooking spray.

2. Put the carrots, onion, mushrooms, ginger, garlic, soy sauce, and broth in the slow cooker. Add 4 cups of water and the chicken thighs. Cook on High for 8 hours.

3. Transfer the chicken to a bowl and shred the meat with two forks. Set aside.

4. When ready to serve, carefully strain the broth into a large saucepan. Remove the mushrooms from the strainer, quarter them, and set aside.

5. Bring the broth to a boil over medium heat. Add the soba noodles and cook for about 4 minutes. Use tongs to transfer the noodles to a strainer and rinse under cold water to stop the cooking process. Add the bok choy to the boiling broth and cook for 2 minutes.

6. To serve, divide the noodles among four bowls, top with chicken, bamboo shoots, baby corn, the mushrooms, and some scallions. Ladle the broth and bok choy over the top. Cut the boiled eggs in half and serve on top of the noodles. Drizzle with chile oil, if desired.

NOTES

Place the eggs in a small pot of salted water. Bring to a boil. As soon as the water comes to a boil, time the eggs for 3 minutes while keeping the water boiling. Remove, peel while hot, and use as directed.

Slow Cooker Pork Chops

Yield: Serves 4 | Prep Time: 15 minutes | Cook Time: 7 to 8 hours on Low or 3½ to 4 hours on High

Canned soups add flavor to the most basic of recipes. I love to stock up on different types when they go on sale and keep a supply of my favorites ready to use for recipes just like this. Feel free to substitute your favorite soup flavors.

INGREDIENTS

4 pork chops, boneless or bone-in

1 teaspoon kosher salt

½ teaspoon freshly ground black pepper

½ teaspoon paprika

1 tablespoon olive oil

¾ cup beef broth

1 (10.75-ounce) can cream of mushroom soup

1 (10.75-ounce) can cream of celery soup

2 teaspoons Worcestershire sauce

1 small onion, sliced

2 garlic cloves, minced

2 cups cremini mushrooms, sliced

2 teaspoons chopped fresh rosemary or thyme

Cooked rice, for serving

Thyme sprigs, for garnish

DIRECTIONS

1. Lightly spray the insert of a 6-quart slow cooker with cooking spray.

2. Season the pork chops with the salt, pepper, and paprika.

3. In a large skillet, heat the olive oil over medium heat. Add the pork chops and cook until brown, about 3 minutes on each side. Transfer the pork chops to a plate.

4. In a large bowl, whisk together the broth, cream of mushroom soup, cream of celery soup, and Worcestershire sauce until combined.

5. Layer the onion, garlic, and mushrooms in the slow cooker.

6. Top with the pork chops, then the soup mixture.

7. Sprinkle with the rosemary.

8. Cover and cook on Low for 7 to 8 hours or on High for 3½ to 4 hours.

9. Serve over rice, garnished with thyme.

General Tso's Chicken

Yield: Serves 4 to 6 | Prep Time: 15 minutes | Cook Time: 4½ hours on Low and 30 minutes on High

We love going to a local Chinese food restaurant on the weekend. The smells and tastes are always so inviting, and re-creating them at home is just as fun. A little bit sweet and a little bit spicy, this chicken dinner brings your takeout favorite home.

INGREDIENTS

2½ pounds boneless, skinless chicken breasts or thighs, or a combination, cut into 1½-inch cubes

½ cup chicken broth

3 tablespoons hoisin sauce

2 tablespoons soy sauce

½ cup packed light brown sugar

3 tablespoons ketchup

1 teaspoon minced fresh ginger

1 teaspoon minced fresh garlic

1 teaspoon sriracha, or more to taste

½ teaspoon red pepper flakes

¼ teaspoon sesame oil

1 tablespoon cornstarch

2 tablespoons water or chicken broth

Cooked white rice, for serving

1 tablespoon toasted sesame seeds, for garnish

1 scallion, sliced, for garnish

DIRECTIONS

1. Spray the insert of a 6-quart slow cooker with cooking spray.

2. In a large bowl, combine the chicken breasts, broth, hoisin sauce, soy sauce, brown sugar, ketchup, ginger, garlic, sriracha, red pepper flakes, and sesame oil and stir to mix well. Place in the slow cooker, cover, and cook on Low for 4½ hours.

3. In a small bowl, stir together the cornstarch and water or broth until smooth. Stir into the chicken mixture, cover, and cook on High for 20 to 30 minutes more, until the sauce thickens.

4. Serve over white rice and garnish each serving with a sprinkle of sesame seeds and scallion.

Mississippi Chicken

Yield: Serves 6 | Prep Time: 5 minutes | Cook Time: 4 to 5 hours on Low or 2 to 2½ hours on High

Southern cooking is some of the best cooking around, which is why this Mississippi Chicken is a must-try. Mississippi Chicken and roast recipes are special because they include pepperoncini, giving them a spicy kick.

INGREDIENTS

3 pounds boneless, skinless chicken thighs

1 onion, coarsely chopped

1 (1-ounce) packet ranch dressing mix

1 (1-ounce) packet au jus gravy mix or brown gravy mix

4 tablespoons (½ stick) unsalted butter, sliced

½ cup chicken broth

7–8 whole pepperoncini

3 cups cooked wild rice, for serving

DIRECTIONS

1. Lightly spray the insert of a 6-quart slow cooker with cooking spray.

2. Lay the chicken thighs along the bottom of the slow cooker.

3. Add the chopped onion on top, then sprinkle the ranch dressing mix and gravy mix on top.

4. Arrange the butter on the top of the chicken. Pour the broth on top.

5. Top with the pepperoncini.

6. Cook on Low for 4 to 5 hours or on High for 2 to 2½ hours.

7. Serve over wild rice.

Orange Chicken

Yield: Serves 4 to 6 | Prep Time: 20 minutes | Cook Time: 4 to 5 hours on Low or 2 to 3 hours on High

This sweet 'n' sticky chicken favorite is a glammed-up version of chicken nuggets. Instead of dipping the bite-size pieces in a pool of ketchup with your fingers, all you need is a fork with all the sauce in this dish.

INGREDIENTS

1 teaspoon rice vinegar

2 tablespoons soy sauce

½ teaspoon toasted sesame oil

1 teaspoon ground ginger, or ½ teaspoon minced fresh ginger

¼ teaspoon red pepper flakes

2 tablespoons scallions, thinly sliced, plus more for garnish

¾ cup orange marmalade

3 tablespoons light brown sugar

½ teaspoon kosher salt

Pinch of freshly ground black pepper

3–4 boneless, skinless chicken breasts, cut into 1½-inch pieces

3 tablespoons cornstarch

2 tablespoons vegetable oil

2–3 cups cooked rice, for serving

DIRECTIONS

1. Spray the insert of a 6-quart slow cooker with cooking spray.

2. In a large bowl, combine the vinegar, soy sauce, sesame oil, ginger, red pepper flakes, scallions, orange marmalade, brown sugar, salt, and black pepper.

3. Put the chicken in a large zip-top plastic bag, add the cornstarch, and shake to coat.

4. In a large skillet, heat the vegetable oil over medium heat. Add the chicken and sear until brown, about 4 minutes on each side.

5. Transfer the chicken to the slow cooker.

6. Pour the sauce over the chicken and stir to combine.

7. Cook on Low for 4 to 5 hours or on High for 2 to 3 hours.

8. Serve with rice, garnished with scallions.

Ranch Bacon Chicken Dinner

Yield: Serves 6 | Prep Time: 10 minutes | Cook Time: 8 hours on Low or 4 to 5 hours on High

I love repurposing dressing mixes when I'm cooking. Ranch is one of my favorites to play around with because it adds loads of flavor without my having to combine a bunch of different spices. Plus, when it's paired with bacon, it makes even the simplest recipes irresistible.

INGREDIENTS

1½ pounds boneless, skinless chicken breasts

4 cups quartered red or Yukon Gold potatoes

2 cups fresh green beans, trimmed

1 (1-ounce) packet ranch dressing mix

2 bacon slices, chopped

4 tablespoons (½ stick) unsalted butter

½ cup chicken broth

DIRECTIONS

1. Lightly spray the insert of a 6-quart slow cooker with cooking spray.

2. Place the chicken in the slow cooker and top with the potatoes and green beans.

3. Top with the ranch dressing mix, bacon, butter, and broth.

4. Cover and cook on Low for 8 hours or on High for 4 to 5 hours.

5. Serve.

French Onion Pork Chops

Yield: Serves 4 | Prep Time: 10 minutes | Cook Time: 3¼ hours

The salty broth mixed with the silky onions adds a comforting touch to this pork chop recipe. When you're coming in from a blustery, chilly day, there's nothing like filling comfort food to make your day that much better.

INGREDIENTS

4 boneless pork chops (¾ inch thick)

½ teaspoon smoked paprika

½ teaspoon coarsely ground black pepper

1 tablespoon olive oil

1 (10.5-ounce) can condensed French onion soup

½ cup white wine or water

2 tablespoons cornstarch

½ cup heavy cream or half-and-half

DIRECTIONS

1. Spray the insert of a 6-quart slow cooker with cooking spray.

2. Sprinkle the pork chops with the paprika and pepper.

3. In a large skillet, heat the olive oil over medium-high heat. When hot, add the pork chops and cook until golden brown on one side, about 5 minutes.

4. Arrange the pork chops in the bottom of the slow cooker and pour the French onion soup and wine over them. Cover and cook on High for 3 hours.

5. In a small bowl, combine the cornstarch and 1 tablespoon water and stir to make a smooth paste, then stir the cornstarch slurry into the cream. Stir the cream mixture into the juices in the slow cooker, cover, and cook on High for 15 minutes more, until slightly thickened.

6. Spoon the gravy on top of the pork chops and serve.

NOTES

Mashed potatoes (page 159) and green beans make excellent sides!

Slow Cooker Chicken Breast with Stuffing

Yield: Serves 4 | Prep Time: 15 minutes | Cook Time: 5 to 5½ hours on Low or 3 to 3½ hours on High

Stuffing has a reputation for being a Thanksgiving-only dish, but there's no reason why you can't enjoy it all year-round. When paired with chicken, it has all the makings of a homemade comfort classic.

INGREDIENTS

1 (12-ounce) package herb-seasoned stuffing mix

1 cup finely chopped onion

1 cup finely chopped celery

1 tablespoon unsalted butter, melted, plus 2 tablespoons unsalted butter, at room temperature

½ teaspoon poultry seasoning

1 teaspoon fresh thyme leaves, plus more for garnish

2 cups chicken broth

¼ teaspoon ground sage

½ teaspoon chopped dried rosemary leaves, plus more for garnish

4 large bone-in, skin-on chicken breasts

DIRECTIONS

1. Spray the insert of a 6-quart slow cooker with cooking spray.

2. In a large bowl, stir together the stuffing mix, onion, celery, melted butter, ¼ teaspoon of the poultry seasoning, and the thyme.

3. In a microwaveable bowl, heat the broth for 2 minutes in the microwave and stir into the mixture in the stuffing mix. Transfer the stuffing mix to the slow cooker.

4. In a small bowl, combine the room-temperature butter with the remaining ¼ teaspoon of the poultry seasoning, the sage, and the rosemary.

5. Loosen the skin from the chicken breasts and use your fingers to spread some of the seasoned butter under the skin. Rub the remaining butter over the top of the chicken pieces.

6. Cover and cook on Low for 5 to 5½ hours or on High for 3 to 3½ hours.

7. Serve warm, garnished with fresh thyme and rosemary.

6-Ingredient Sriracha Chicken

Yield: Serves 4 │ Prep Time: 10 minutes │ Cook Time: 5 hours on Low or 2½ hours on High

Sweet, spicy, salty—this dish has it all. I love making this chicken and serving it many different ways throughout the week. It's the most versatile chicken around and perfect to top a pizza, stuff in a bun, or mix into a salad.

INGREDIENTS

4 boneless, skinless chicken breasts

½ cup honey

½ cup sriracha

½ cup soy sauce

1 tablespoon minced garlic

1 red bell pepper, sliced into 1-inch pieces

Cooked brown rice, for serving

DIRECTIONS

1. Spray the insert of a 6-quart slow cooker with cooking spray.

2. Lay the chicken breasts in the slow cooker in a single layer.

3. In a small bowl, stir together the honey, sriracha, soy sauce, and garlic. Pour over the chicken. Add the bell pepper. Cover and cook on Low for 5 hours or on High for 2½ hours.

4. Serve the chicken and sauce over brown rice.

Beef and Broccoli

Yield: Serves 4 | Prep Time: 15 minutes | Cook Time: 3¼ hours

Broccoli is so good for you, so the more times I can add it to a recipe, the better! The juicy beef roast simply melts in your mouth with every bite and that broccoli crunch gives the spoonful a great texture.

INGREDIENTS

1 pound beef chuck roast

1 cup beef broth

½ cup soy sauce

2 tablespoons light brown sugar

1 tablespoon hoisin sauce

1 tablespoon toasted sesame oil

1 tablespoon minced garlic

1 tablespoon minced fresh ginger

2 tablespoons cornstarch

2 cups frozen broccoli florets, thawed

Cooked white rice, for serving

Sesame seeds, for garnish

DIRECTIONS

1. Spray the insert of a 6-quart slow cooker with cooking spray.

2. Cut the beef into ¼-inch-thick slices and then into strips about 1 × 3 inches and place them in the slow cooker.

3. In a medium bowl, combine the broth, soy sauce, brown sugar, hoisin sauce, sesame oil, garlic, and ginger and stir until the sugar has dissolved. Pour over the beef in the slow cooker and toss to coat. Cover and cook on Low for 3 hours.

4. In a small bowl, combine the cornstarch and 2 tablespoons water to make a slurry. Stir the cornstarch slurry into the juices in the slow cooker, then add the broccoli. Cover and cook on Low for 15 minutes more.

5. Serve over white rice, garnished with sesame seeds.

Chicken Fried Rice

Yield: Serves 6 to 8 | Prep Time: 10 minutes | Cook Time: 3 hours

Talk about comfort food. I remember ordering Chicken Fried Rice in college and sitting on the floor eating it with friends after a late night out. Now when I'm serving it at home, I truly appreciate all the flavors that go into it! Cooking with fresh ginger gives this dish a tangy freshness and mellow sweetness that make it an unforgettable cure to any fatigue.

INGREDIENTS

1 pound boneless, skinless chicken breasts or thighs, or a combination, cut into 1-inch cubes

⅓ cup soy sauce

2 tablespoons rice vinegar

1 tablespoon sesame oil

1 tablespoon minced garlic

2 teaspoons minced fresh ginger

2 cups jasmine rice

3 cups chicken broth

2 cups frozen peas and carrots, thawed

4 scallions, slivered

DIRECTIONS

1. Spray the insert of a 6-quart slow cooker with cooking spray.

2. Put the chicken in a medium bowl.

3. In a small bowl, combine the soy sauce, vinegar, sesame oil, garlic, and ginger. Pour about half the soy sauce mixture over the chicken and toss to coat. Place the chicken over the bottom of the slow cooker.

4. Spread the rice over the chicken and add the broth. Cover and cook on High for 2½ hours.

5. Add the peas and carrots and the remaining soy sauce mixture and toss well. Cover and cook for 30 minutes more, or until the rice is completely cooked.

6. Toss again before serving. Garnish with the scallions.

Honey Mustard Chicken and Broccoli

Yield: Serves 4 | Prep Time: 25 minutes | Cook Time: 3¼ hours

Although this dish sounds simple, the reason it is so delicious is because it cooks low and slow and the brown sugar gets trapped under the chicken breast skin, which makes the chicken soak up extra flavor.

INGREDIENTS

1 orange

2 tablespoons maple syrup

1½ tablespoons Dijon mustard

2 teaspoons minced garlic

½ teaspoon kosher salt

4 large bone-in, skin-on chicken thighs

4 teaspoons light brown sugar

1 tablespoon vegetable oil

1 tablespoon white wine or white wine vinegar

8 ounces fresh broccoli florets

DIRECTIONS

1. Spray the insert of a 6-quart slow cooker with cooking spray.

2. Zest half the orange and then squeeze the juice from that half. Place the zest and juice in a small bowl and cut the remaining orange half into wedges to be used for garnish; set aside.

3. Add the maple syrup, mustard, garlic, and salt to the bowl with the orange zest and juice and stir to mix well. Set aside.

4. Trim any excess fat from the chicken thighs and use your fingers to separate the skin from the meat. Slide 1 teaspoon of the brown sugar under the skin of each thigh and spread it evenly.

5. In a large nonstick skillet, heat the vegetable oil over medium-high heat. Place the chicken in the skillet, skin-side down, and cook for 4 minutes, until golden. Transfer the chicken to the slow cooker and arrange the thighs skin-side up.

6. Drain off all but 1 teaspoon of the oil from the skillet and return it to medium-high heat. Pour in the wine and stir to scrape up any browned bits stuck to the bottom of the pan. Add the maple syrup mixture and cook, stirring, until the sauce begins to thicken and boil. Pour over the chicken in the slow cooker, cover, and cook on High for 3 hours.

7. Separate the broccoli florets and lay them over the chicken in the slow cooker. Cover and cook on High until the broccoli is steamed to crisp-tender, 15 to 20 minutes.

8. Serve, garnished with the reserved orange wedges.

Lemon Pepper Salmon

Yield: Serves 4 | Prep Time: 15 minutes | Cook Time: 1 to 1½ hours

Salmon is my tried and true healthy dinner. It's satisfying, but a feel-good meal. The spices in this recipe are subtle and don't overpower the dish, making for the perfect light weeknight meal.

INGREDIENTS

2 lemons

1 large onion, thinly sliced

2 pounds salmon fillets, all bones removed

1 small bay leaf

2 teaspoons lemon pepper, plus more for garnish (optional)

2 cups chicken broth

Tartar sauce, for serving

DIRECTIONS

1. Spray the insert of a 6-quart slow cooker with cooking spray. Set the slow cooker to preheat on High while you assemble the recipe.

2. Halve one of the lemons and thinly slice one half. Place the onion and lemon slices in an even layer over the bottom of the slow cooker.

3. Lay the salmon fillets, skin-side down, in one layer over the vegetables and tuck in the bay leaf. Sprinkle liberally with lemon pepper and squeeze the juice of the lemon half over the salmon.

4. Bring the broth to a simmer in a saucepan on the stovetop or in the microwave and gently pour it around the salmon—it should come up the sides of the fillets and not quite cover the top; add water if necessary. Cut a piece of parchment paper to the shape and size of your slow cooker so that it just fits inside. Lay it lightly on top of the fish, cover the slow cooker, and cook on High for 1 to 1½ hours, depending on the thickness of the fillets.

5. Use a flat spatula to remove the salmon and serve immediately or let cool completely (discard the bay leaf and vegetables). If serving immediately, cut the remaining lemon into wheels to garnish and serve with the fish, along with tartar sauce. Sprinkle with extra lemon pepper before serving, if desired.

Shredded Chicken Tacos

Yield: Serves 5 | Prep Time: 5 minutes | Cook Time: 6 to 8 hours on Low or 4 to 6 hours on High

Who doesn't look forward to taco night? This Mexican-style favorite substitutes chicken for the more traditional ground beef. Don't forget to load up on toppings! Tomatoes, lettuce, guacamole, and of course a little cheese and sour cream are my preferred toppings.

INGREDIENTS

1½ pounds boneless, skinless chicken breasts

1 (10-ounce) can Ro-Tel tomatoes

1 (1-ounce) packet taco seasoning mix

1 (14-ounce) can low-sodium chicken broth

Soft taco shells, for serving

Your favorite taco toppings: jalapeños, lettuce, tomatoes, shredded cheddar cheese, olives, sour cream, guacamole, fresh lime, cilantro, and hot sauce, as desired

DIRECTIONS

1. Lightly spray a 6-quart slow cooker with cooking spray.

2. Place the chicken over the bottom of the slow cooker in a single layer.

3. Meanwhile, in a bowl, mix the tomatoes, taco seasoning, and broth. Pour the mixture over the chicken. Cover and cook on Low for 6 to 8 hours or on High for 4 to 6 hours, until the chicken shreds easily.

4. Transfer the chicken to a bowl and shred the meat.

5. Serve in soft taco shells with your favorite toppings.

Teriyaki Chicken

Yield: Serves 6 to 8 | Prep Time: 20 minutes | Cook Time: 3¼ hours

The subtle sweetness of this sauce with the crunch of the red quinoa make this a memorable dish. The white rice gives the recipe a traditional flair, while the quinoa adds a healthier twist.

INGREDIENTS

1½ pounds boneless, skinless chicken breasts, cut into 1½-inch pieces

¼ cup honey

⅓ cup soy sauce

¼ cup rice vinegar

1 teaspoon toasted sesame oil

½ teaspoon minced fresh garlic

½ teaspoon minced fresh ginger

2 cups red quinoa

2 cups chicken broth

3–4 scallions, cut into 1-inch-long pieces

1 red bell pepper, cut into 1-inch squares

1 green bell pepper, cut into 1-inch squares

1 cup canned pineapple chunks, drained

2 tablespoons cornstarch, mixed with 2 tablespoons water

Cooked white or brown rice, for serving

Slivered scallions, for garnish

DIRECTIONS

1. Spray the insert of a 6-quart slow cooker with cooking spray.

2. Place the chicken in the slow cooker.

3. In a medium bowl, stir together the honey, soy sauce, vinegar, sesame oil, garlic, and ginger. Pour the mixture over the chicken.

4. Rinse the red quinoa under cool water until loose and separated and add to the slow cooker along with the broth; stir briefly.

5. Scatter the scallions and bell peppers over the chicken.

6. Cover and cook on High for 3 hours.

7. Stir in the pineapple and the cornstarch-water mixture, cover, and cook for 15 minutes more or until the sauce has thickened.

8. Serve over rice, garnished with slivers of scallion.

5

Side Dish Recipes

I hate having to choose what kind of dish gets first dibs on oven space.
Between roasts and side dish casseroles and desserts like pies and cakes,
there's simply not enough room for them all. When I have my slow
cooker handy, however, I don't have to choose. I can simply pop my
favorite side into the slow cooker to free up my oven for other options.

Au Gratin Potatoes

Yield: Serves 8 | Prep Time: 20 minutes | Cook Time: 2½ to 3 hours

During the holidays, when the entire kitchen is in chaos, this cheesy dish can be quietly cooking off on the side, out of the way of everything else. Use Yukon Gold potatoes for the fluffiest texture, and the sour cream and cheese with the nutmeg gives it all the flavor you need.

INGREDIENTS

2 pounds Yukon Gold potatoes, peeled and thinly sliced (about 5 cups)

1 teaspoon kosher salt, plus additional for serving

1 teaspoon freshly ground pepper, plus additional for serving

1 tablespoon slivered garlic

4 tablespoons (½ stick) unsalted butter, plus additional for serving

¼ cup all-purpose flour

1½ cups whole milk

½ cup sour cream

½ teaspoon freshly grated nutmeg

6 ounces white cheddar cheese, shredded just before using

Fresh thyme, for garnish

DIRECTIONS

1. Spray the insert of a 6-quart slow cooker with cooking spray.

2. Make three layers of potatoes in the slow cooker, with one-third of the salt, pepper, and garlic between each layer and on top.

3. In a medium saucepan, melt the butter over medium heat. Whisk in the flour and cook, stirring, for 2 minutes, until the mixture turns light yellow and large bubbles form. Slowly whisk in the milk and cook, whisking continuously, for 2 to 3 minutes, until the sauce thickens. Remove from the heat. Stir in the sour cream and nutmeg and gradually stir in the cheese until completely melted and smooth.

4. Pour the sauce over the potatoes, spreading it evenly to cover all. Do not stir.

5. Place three long pieces of paper towel over the top of the slow cooker and cover with the lid. Cook on High for 2½ hours. Uncover and check the potatoes: the edges should be golden brown and the potatoes should be tender. If they're not tender, cover and cook for 15 minutes more.

6. Remove the lid and paper towels and cook on High, uncovered, for 15 minutes more. Let stand for about 15 minutes before serving.

7. Serve warm, with thyme, butter, salt, and pepper.

DIY Baked Potatoes

Yield: Serves 6 to 8 | Prep Time: 10 minutes | Cook Time: 8 hours on Low or 4 hours on High

I like setting up a topping bar when I bake potatoes, so everyone can pile on the sour cream, bacon, scallions, or whatever else they may want. By making potatoes in the slow cooker, I have plenty of room in the oven to cook up fries and mozzarella sticks for an appetizer feast.

INGREDIENTS

6–8 russet potatoes (about 10 ounces each)

6–8 teaspoons olive oil

Kosher salt and freshly ground black pepper

Sour cream, for serving

Sliced scallions, for serving

Crumbled cooked bacon, for serving

DIRECTIONS

1. Cut six to eight squares of aluminum foil large enough to wrap each potato completely.

2. Scrub and dry the potatoes very well. Set each potato on a square of foil, drizzle with 1 teaspoon of the olive oil, and rub to evenly coat. Sprinkle with salt and pepper and pierce with a fork all over. Seal each potato in the foil.

3. Pour ½ cup water into a 6-quart slow cooker, then transfer the wrapped potatoes to the slow cooker. Cover and cook on Low for 8 hours or on High for 4 hours, until the potatoes are tender.

4. Serve with sour cream, scallions, and bacon.

Buttery Corn on the Cob

Yield: Serves 4 | Prep Time: 10 minutes | Cook Time: 2 hours

I love corn on the cob, and my motto is the more buttery, the better. Be sure to have corn holders handy so you can dig in without burning your fingers.

INGREDIENTS

3 tablespoons unsalted butter, melted

½ teaspoon kosher salt, plus more as needed

¼ teaspoon freshly ground black pepper, plus more as needed

4 ears corn on the cob

DIRECTIONS

1. Spray the insert of a 6-quart slow cooker with cooking spray. Cut four squares of aluminum foil large enough to wrap each ear of corn completely.

2. In a small bowl, combine the butter, salt, and pepper and brush the butter over all surfaces of the corn. Wrap each ear of corn in a square of foil, twisting the ends to seal. Place in the slow cooker, leaving room for heat to circulate between the ears if possible, cover, and cook on Low for 2 hours.

3. Remove the foil, season with salt and pepper, and serve.

Creamed Corn

When I use the slow cooker to make Creamed Corn, the sauce stays creamy and ready to eat because I can simply set the slow cooker on Warm and not worry about the sauce thickening as it cools.

INGREDIENTS

1 pound frozen corn kernels (4 cups)

1 (8-ounce) package cream cheese, at room temperature

½ cup half-and-half

½ cup (1 stick) unsalted butter, cut into pieces

2 tablespoons maple syrup

1 teaspoon kosher salt

1 teaspoon freshly ground black pepper, plus more as needed

Fresh parsley, for garnish

DIRECTIONS

1. Spray the insert of a 6-quart slow cooker with cooking spray.

2. Put the corn, cream cheese, half-and-half, butter, maple syrup, salt, and pepper in the slow cooker. Do not worry about combining everything perfectly, as it will melt together as it cooks. Cover and cook on High for 2 hours, stirring halfway through the cooking time.

3. With an immersion blender, carefully blend the hot mixture to the desired consistency directly in the slow cooker.

4. Serve with plenty of freshly ground black pepper and fresh parsley.

Creamy Mashed Potatoes

Yield: Serves 6 to 8 | Prep Time: 10 minutes | Cook Time: 4 to 5 hours

Everyone has their particular preferences when it comes to mashed potatoes. I love mine un-peeled and super creamy. The smooth texture comes from the cream cheese. It's a super-fun way to add flavor and texture to the classic.

INGREDIENTS

5 pounds Yukon Gold potatoes, unpeeled, cut into 1-inch pieces

Kosher salt and freshly ground black pepper

1 cup (2 sticks) unsalted butter, cut into small pieces

1 (8-ounce) package cream cheese, at room temperature

3–4 tablespoons whole milk

Fresh thyme, for garnish

DIRECTIONS

1. Spray the insert of a 6-quart slow cooker with cooking spray.

2. Rinse the potato pieces in cold water and place them in the slow cooker. Season with salt and pepper. Pour in 3 cups of water, then sprinkle ¼ cup of the butter pieces across the top of the potatoes.

3. Cover and cook the potatoes on High for 4 to 5 hours, until the potatoes are fork-tender.

4. Carefully drain into a colander. Return the potatoes to the slow cooker. Add the remaining butter and the cream cheese. Mash the potatoes with a potato masher until they reach the desired consistency. Add the milk to thin the potatoes as needed. Taste and season with additional salt and pepper.

5. Serve hot, garnished with fresh thyme.

Honey-Glazed Carrots

Yield: Serves 6 to 8 | Prep Time: 10 minutes | Cook Time: 3 hours

I always tell my friends that this recipe is a great way to sneak vegetables into their kids' diets. The honey glaze and orange tang make these carrots taste like candy, but the bold flavor from the horseradish keeps them slightly sophisticated and packed with flavor for the adults.

INGREDIENTS

2 pounds carrots, cut into 1½-inch pieces

¼ cup honey

4 tablespoons (½ stick) unsalted butter, melted

¼ cup prepared horseradish

½ teaspoon kosher salt

2 tablespoons orange juice concentrate, undiluted

Fresh parsley, for garnish

DIRECTIONS

1. Spray the insert of a 6-quart slow cooker with cooking spray.

2. Place the carrots in the slow cooker.

3. In a small bowl, combine the honey, butter, horseradish, salt, and orange juice concentrate and pour over the carrots. Cover and cook on High for 3 hours, stirring once after 2 hours.

4. Serve garnished with fresh parsley.

Country-Style Baked Beans

Yield: Serves 6 | Prep Time: 20 minutes | Cook Time: 4 hours on Low or 2 hours on High

When you think of baked beans, you might think of a BBQ, but these aren't your average baked beans. They're full of country-style ingredients such as barbecue sauce and brown sugar. This dish is a hearty favorite fit for the best barbecue or block party in town.

INGREDIENTS

6 bacon slices, chopped

1½ cups barbecue sauce

⅓ cup packed light brown sugar

1 (15-ounce) can chili beans, drained

1 (15-ounce) can navy beans, drained and rinsed

1 (15½-ounce) can butter beans, drained and rinsed

1 (16-ounce) can pork and beans, not drained

Fresh parsley, for garnish

DIRECTIONS

1. Spray the insert of a 6-quart slow cooker with cooking spray.

2. In a small skillet, cook the bacon over medium heat until crisp. Drain on paper towels. Set aside.

3. In the slow cooker, combine the barbecue sauce, brown sugar, and ½ cup water and mix well. Stir in the chili beans, navy beans, butter beans, pork and beans, and bacon. Cover and cook on Low for 4 hours or on High for 2 hours.

4. Serve immediately, garnished with fresh parsley.

Mac 'n' Cheese

Yield: Serves 6 | Prep Time: 20 minutes | Cook Time: 2 hours

Whenever I see a buffet spread, I like to hit up the mac 'n' cheese first to make sure I don't run out of valuable plate real estate. This mac 'n' cheese dish has a hint of paprika, giving it a smoky flavor. It's a fun twist on the traditional version I remember from being a kid.

INGREDIENTS

1 (16-ounce) box cellentani, cavatappi, or fusilli pasta

3 cups whole milk

8 ounces Velveeta cheese, cut into 1-inch cubes

4 tablespoons (½ stick) unsalted butter, cut into cubes

¼ teaspoon smoked paprika, plus more for garnish

3 cups shredded cheddar cheese

⅓ cup grated Parmesan cheese

DIRECTIONS

1. Spray the insert of a 6-quart slow cooker with cooking spray.

2. Bring a large pot of water to a boil. Add the pasta and cook until about 90% cooked. It will finish cooking in the slow cooker. Drain well.

3. Place the noodles in the slow cooker. Top with the remaining ingredients. Cook on Low for 2 hours.

4. Remove the lid and stir to combine. Sprinkle with additional paprika and serve warm.

Slow Cooker Stuffing

Yield: Serves 4 to 6 | Prep Time: 10 minutes | Cook Time: 4 to 5 hours

Stuffing doesn't have to stay locked up in your recipe arsenal until Thanksgiving rolls around. It's just as yummy to make on the side of chicken or pork chops as it is with turkey. Plus, with this slow cooker version, you won't have to worry about taking up valuable stovetop space.

INGREDIENTS

12 cups dry marbled rye bread cubes

2 cups chopped celery (about 4 stalks)

1 onion, sliced

1 carrot, chopped

2 tablespoons oregano

½ teaspoon salt

¼ teaspoon black pepper

1¾ cups chicken broth

⅓ cup butter, melted

DIRECTIONS

1. In a large bowl, combine the bread cubes, celery, onion, carrot, oregano, salt, and pepper. Pour the chicken broth and melted butter over the bread mixture; toss to mix well.

2. Pour the mixture in a 6-quart slow cooker. Cover and cook for 4 to 5 hours on Low. Serve warm.

Corn Bread

Yield: Serves 6 to 8 | Prep Time: 15 minutes | Cook Time: 2 hours

When you have a roast cooking in the oven and sides cooking on the stovetop, you can complete your Sunday night meal by whipping up this corn bread in the slow cooker. It's a great recipe to bring out around the holidays when your kitchen's in full use.

INGREDIENTS

1½ cups all-purpose flour

1½ cups cornmeal

1 teaspoon kosher salt

½ teaspoon freshly ground black pepper

3 tablespoons sugar

1 tablespoon baking powder

2 cups buttermilk

2 large eggs

2 tablespoons unsalted butter, melted

DIRECTIONS

1. In a large bowl, mix the flour, cornmeal, salt, pepper, sugar, and baking powder.

2. In a separate bowl, mix together the buttermilk and eggs. Pour over the flour mixture and mix until just combined. The batter may be slightly lumpy.

3. Pour the melted butter into the insert of a 6-quart slow cooker. Pour in the corn bread batter and spread it evenly.

4. Place a long piece of paper towel over the top of the slow cooker and cover with the lid. Cook on High for 2 hours.

5. Remove the lid and paper towels and let cool for 20 minutes before cutting into squares and serving.

Pizza Pull-Apart Bread

Yield: Serves 6 | Prep Time: 20 minutes | Cook Time: 1½ hours

Pizza Pull-Apart Bread is a movie night must-have. Whenever I lay out a spread of appetizers, this dish is always the first to go. Feel free to sprinkle some Parmesan cheese and red pepper flakes over the top and forget the frozen pizza routine—this will be your new favorite way to indulge in Pizza 2.0.

INGREDIENTS

¼ cup olive oil

½ teaspoon Italian dry spice mix

1 (16.3-ounce) tube Pillsbury Grands refrigerated rolls

1 (14-ounce) can or jar pizza sauce

3 ounces sliced pepperoni, coarsely chopped

4 ounces shredded mozzarella cheese

Grated Parmesan cheese

Fresh basil, for garnish

DIRECTIONS

1. Line the slow cooker with a piece of parchment paper, leaving an overhang like a sling.

2. In a small bowl, combine the olive oil and spice mix.

3. Pull apart the rolls and cut each into 6 wedges. Using your fingers, stretch and pull each into an approximately 1½-inch square. Spoon about 1 teaspoon of the pizza sauce on each square and top with a piece of pepperoni and 1 teaspoon of the mozzarella. Pull the edges together and pinch to seal completely. Dip into the bowl of olive oil and arrange in the bottom of the slow cooker loosely next to one another. When the bottom is covered, sprinkle with 1 tablespoon of the mozzarella and continue making even layers until all the biscuit pieces have been used. Sprinkle any remaining pepperoni and cheese on top and drizzle with any remaining olive oil.

4. Cover and cook on High for 1½ hours. Serve with the remaining pizza sauce for dipping. Sprinkle with Parmesan cheese and garnish with fresh basil.

Dinner Rolls

Yield: 8 rolls | Prep Time: 15 minutes | Cook Time: 1½ hours

Dinner Rolls can fancy up any kind of supper. When you pull them out, fresh and warm, it's impossible not to be tempted by the buttery, fluffy goodness. Another amazing bread recipe that can be done so easily in the slow cooker, making fresh homemade bread doable!

INGREDIENTS

1 (0.25-ounce) packet rapid-rise yeast

1 teaspoon sugar

1½ cups water, warmed to 120°F

3½ cups plus 3 tablespoons all-purpose flour

¼ teaspoon kosher salt

3 tablespoons unsalted butter, melted

DIRECTIONS

1. In the bowl of a stand mixer fitted with the paddle attachment, combine the yeast and sugar and pour the warm water on top. Stir on low speed for 1 minute. With the machine running, gradually add 3½ cups of the flour and the salt and mix for 3 minutes. Remove the paddle and cover the bowl with plastic wrap and a dish towel. Let rise for 1 hour, until the dough has doubled in size.

2. Dust a work surface with the remaining 3 tablespoons of the flour and scoop the dough onto the surface. Dust your hands with some of the flour and roll the dough into a log. Divide into 8 equal portions and roll each portion into a smooth ball, pinching the bottom seam.

3. Line the bottom of a 6-quart slow cooker insert with a piece of parchment paper cut to fit. (Draw around the lid to get the correct size, cut, and fit into the slow cooker.) Spray very lightly with cooking spray. Fit the dough balls, seam-side down, into the slow cooker in one layer. Cover and cook on High for 1½ hours.

4. When the rolls are cooked, preheat the oven to broil. Transfer the rolls onto a baking sheet. Melt the butter and brush the tops of the rolls well and broil for 8 to 10 minutes, until evenly browned on top. Serve.

6

Soup and Stew Recipes

Soups and stews are instant pick-me-ups. When the weather cools down,
I find myself fantasizing about holding a bowl of something warm
while I snuggle up in my thickest blanket. I love prepping soups and
stews like these in my slow cooker in the morning and smelling them
all day long while I do chores or relax on the couch with my dog.

French Onion Soup

Yield: Serves 6 | Prep Time: 30 minutes | Cook Time: 18 to 20 hours

This recipe takes longer to cook, but it's worth the wait. I like dunking a loaf of crusty bread into the onion soup broth or even adding some croutons for extra crunch. What makes this version so special is that you don't have to continuously stir, like you would if you were to make it on the stovetop. This is an easy way to re-create the classic.

INGREDIENTS

3 pounds onions, sliced

4 tablespoons (½ stick) unsalted butter, melted

2 tablespoons olive oil

1 teaspoon kosher salt

2 teaspoons freshly ground black pepper, plus more as needed

3 fresh thyme sprigs

2 bay leaves

10 cups beef broth

3 tablespoons dry sherry (optional)

12 baguette slices

1 cup shredded Gruyère cheese

DIRECTIONS

1. Spray the insert of a 6-quart slow cooker with cooking spray.

2. Place the onion slices in the slow cooker. Stir in the butter, olive oil, salt, and pepper. Cover and cook on Low for 12 hours. The onions will be golden brown, very fragrant and soft.

3. Stir in the thyme sprigs, bay leaves, beef broth, and sherry, if using. Cover and cook on Low for 6 to 8 hours more.

4. Remove the bay leaves and ladle the soup into crocks.

5. Preheat the broiler. Top the baguette slices generously with cheese and broil for 2 to 3 minutes until the cheese is melted and bubbling.

6. Top each bowl with two slices of toasted bread, sprinkle with pepper, and serve immediately.

Chicken Noodle Soup

Yield: Serves 8 | Prep Time: 10 minutes | Cook Time: 6¼ hours

This is it: the ultimate feel-better soup. Whenever I or my husband is home sick I like to make a batch of slow cooker chicken noodle soup to lift our spirits in the morning. It's amazing how one little dish can go such a long way, and if you are the one under the weather, it is an easy one to make even if you have to do so with a blanket over your shoulders.

INGREDIENTS

1½ pounds boneless, skinless chicken breasts or thighs, or a combination, cut into 1-inch cubes

2 cups finely diced carrots

1 cup finely diced onion

1 cup finely diced celery

1 teaspoon minced garlic

2 tablespoons chopped fresh parsley

1 teaspoon fresh thyme leaves, or ½ teaspoon dried thyme

½ teaspoon poultry seasoning

½ teaspoon kosher salt, plus more to taste

¼ teaspoon freshly ground black pepper, plus more to taste

1 bay leaf

6 cups chicken broth

4 ounces curly wide egg noodles

Sliced scallions, for garnish

DIRECTIONS

1. In a 6-quart slow cooker, combine the chicken, carrots, onion, celery, garlic, parsley, thyme, poultry seasoning, salt, pepper, and bay leaf. Pour the broth over and stir, then cover and cook on Low for 6 hours.

2. Add the egg noodles, cover, and cook for 10 to 15 minutes more, until the noodles are tender. Remove the bay leaf, taste, and season with salt and pepper as needed.

3. Serve, garnished with scallions.

Chicken Tortilla Soup

Yield: Serves 6 to 8 | Prep Time: 30 minutes | Cook Time: 6 to 8 hours

One reason chicken tortilla soup is so popular is that it is a kicked-up version of good ol' chicken noodle soup. Packed with flavor, this soup has lots of other filling ingredients to offer, but the salty, crunchy topping of tortilla chips will always be part of what makes me love it so much.

INGREDIENTS

1 (10-ounce) can enchilada sauce

1 (12-ounce) can Ro-Tel tomatoes

1 (14-ounce) can black beans, drained and rinsed

1 (10-ounce) package frozen corn

1 onion, chopped

1 (14.5-ounce) can low-sodium chicken broth

1 teaspoon ground cumin

1 teaspoon chili powder

Kosher salt and freshly ground black pepper

1 pound boneless, skinless chicken breasts

Tortilla chips, for serving

Lime wedges, for serving

DIRECTIONS

1. In a 6-quart slow cooker, combine the enchilada sauce, tomatoes, black beans, corn, onion, broth, cumin, chili powder, 2 cups of water, and salt and pepper to taste. Stir to combine with a large spoon.

2. Nestle the chicken breasts into the soup mixture. Cover and cook on Low for 6 to 8 hours.

3. When ready to serve, transfer the chicken to a large bowl and shred the meat with two forks. Return the chicken to the slow cooker and stir to combine.

4. Serve in large bowls topped with tortilla chips. Squeeze a wedge of lime over each serving.

Budget-Friendly Chicken Stew

Yield: Serves 6 | Prep Time: 20 minutes | Cook Time: 6½ hours

The trickiest part about making homemade soups and stews is how pricey they can become. Soups and stews tend to have lots of ingredients, which can turn into a big grocery bill. This recipe works well because not only does it use inexpensive chicken thighs, but it also uses fewer than ten (inexpensive!) ingredients, allowing you to stay well within your grocery budget.

INGREDIENTS

6 boneless, skinless chicken thighs

1 (16-ounce) can kidney beans, drained and rinsed

1 (16-ounce) can low-sodium chicken broth

3–4 Yukon Gold potatoes, diced

2 carrots, sliced

1 bay leaf

2 cups chopped kale

Kosher salt and freshly ground black pepper

DIRECTIONS

1. Spray the insert of a 6-quart slow cooker with cooking spray.

2. Place the chicken, kidney beans, chicken broth, potatoes, carrots, and bay leaf in the slow cooker. Cover and cook on Low for 6 hours.

3. Add the kale, remove the bay leaf, and cook on Low for 30 minutes more.

4. Season with salt and pepper and serve warm.

Cheeseburger Soup

Yield: Serves 8 | Prep Time: 15 minutes | Cook Time: 6½ to 8½ hours on Low or 4½ to 5½ hours on High

I love this recipe because it combines all my favorite parts of a burger into a single dish. The potatoes are like a faux fry element, so it's like you're getting a full meal!

INGREDIENTS

4 small potatoes, diced

1 small white or yellow onion, sliced

1 cup shredded carrots

½ cup diced celery

3 cups beef broth

1 pound lean ground beef

3 tablespoons unsalted butter

¼ cup all-purpose flour

2 cups heavy cream

½ teaspoon salt

½ teaspoon black pepper

1 (16-ounce) package Velveeta processed cheese, cubed

DIRECTIONS

1. Place the potatoes, onion, carrots, and celery in a 6-quart slow cooker. Pour the broth over the vegetables. Cover and cook for 6 to 8 hours on Low or for 4 to 5 hours on High until the potatoes are tender.

2. About 45 minutes before serving, crumble and cook the ground beef in a large skillet over medium-high heat. Drain any grease. Pour the cooked ground beef into the slow cooker. Carefully wipe out the hot skillet with a paper towel, then add the butter. When the butter is melted, whisk in the flour and cook until golden brown and bubbly (about 1 minute). Whisk in the cream, salt, and pepper. Pour the mixture into the slow cooker and stir to combine everything.

3. Add the cubed Velveeta cheese to the slow cooker. Stir again. Cover and cook for another 30 minutes or until the cheese is melted. Ladle into bowls and serve.

Minestrone Pasta

Yield: Serves 10 | Prep Time: 15 minutes | Cook Time: 6 to 8 hours on Low or 3 to 4 hours on High, plus an additional 20 to 25 minutes on High

Minestrone soup never tastes as good when it's premade in a can as when you have a homemade batch. And luckily for me and my vegetable drawer, minestrone soup is such a hodgepodge that it's simple to add in other seasonal produce like peas or zucchini as it fits your mood. The Parmesan rind lends the broth lots of extra flavor.

INGREDIENTS

2 (14.5-ounce) cans diced tomatoes

1 (6-ounce) can tomato paste

¼ cup pesto (homemade or store-bought)

1 Parmesan rind

6 cups vegetable stock

1 cup carrots, diced

1¼ cups celery, diced

1½ cups white onion, diced

4–5 cloves garlic

1 teaspoon dried oregano

Salt and pepper to taste

1 (15-ounce) can red kidney beans, drained and rinsed

1 (15-ounce) can great northern beans, drained and rinsed

1½ cups ditalini pasta

DIRECTIONS

1. In a 6-quart slow cooker, place the diced tomatoes, tomato paste, pesto, Parmesan rind, vegetable stock, carrots, celery, onion, garlic, and oregano. Season with salt and pepper to taste. Cover and cook for 6 to 8 hours on Low or for 3 to 4 hours on High.

2. Add in the red kidney beans, great northern beans, and ditalini pasta, cover, and cook for an additional 20 to 25 minutes on High until the pasta is tender. Remove the rind and serve warm.

Hungarian Goulash

Yield: Serves 4 | Prep Time: 20 minutes | Cook Time: 6½ to 8½ hours

There are so many different ways to cook goulash, whether you decide to add extra onion or a couple of different types of bell peppers or new spices you have in your cabinet. This is my version of the dish, inspired by the Old World–style recipes from Central Europe.

INGREDIENTS

1 tablespoon olive oil

2 pounds beef stew meat, cut into 1-inch cubes

1 garlic clove, minced

3–4 Yukon Gold potatoes, cut into ½-inch cubes

½ cup ketchup

2 tablespoons Worcestershire sauce

2 teaspoons kosher salt

1 tablespoon paprika

1 (10-ounce) bag frozen mixed peas, corn, and carrots

1 (12-ounce) bag egg noodles

Fresh parsley, for garnish

DIRECTIONS

1. In a large heavy-bottomed pot, heat the olive oil over medium heat. Add the beef and sear the meat until browned on all sides. Do not worry about cooking it completely, just browning the outsides. Transfer the beef to a 6-quart slow cooker.

2. Add the garlic, potatoes, ketchup, Worcestershire sauce, salt, and paprika. Stir to combine.

3. Add 1 cup of water, cover, and cook on Low for 6 to 8 hours. The meat will be tender and the sauce will have thickened.

4. Add the frozen vegetables and cook for 30 minutes more.

5. Meanwhile, bring a large pot of water to a boil. Add the egg noodles and cook until al dente according to the package directions. Drain and set aside until ready to serve.

6. Serve the goulash over the cooked noodles, garnished with parsley.

Potato Soup

Yield: Serves 8 | Prep Time: 15 minutes | Cook Time: 6 hours on Low or 4 hours on High

There are few dishes that beat a hearty, rich potato soup. The potato chunks simply melt in your mouth, while the chunks of bacon add a savory twist.

INGREDIENTS

2–3 bacon slices

1 tablespoon unsalted butter

1 cup chopped onion

1 tablespoon minced garlic

3 pounds red or Yukon Gold potatoes, peeled, if desired, and cut into ½-inch cubes

6 cups chicken broth

2 tablespoons coarsely chopped fresh chives

½ teaspoon kosher salt

½ teaspoon freshly ground black pepper

1 cup heavy cream, at room temperature

1 cup shredded cheddar cheese, at room temperature

1 cup sour cream, at room temperature

¼ cup finely chopped chives, for garnish

DIRECTIONS

1. Spray the insert of a 7-quart slow cooker with cooking spray.

2. In a small skillet, cook the bacon over medium-high heat until browned but not crisp. Remove the bacon with a slotted spoon and set aside. Drain all but 1 tablespoon of the fat from the skillet and set it over medium heat. Add the butter and onion and cook, stirring frequently, until translucent, about 2 minutes. Stir in the garlic and cook for 1 minute more.

3. Place the potatoes in the slow cooker and pour the onion mixture over them. Add the bacon, broth, chives, salt, and pepper. Cover and cook on Low for 6 hours or on High for 4 hours.

4. Turn off the slow cooker. In a small bowl combine the heavy cream, cheddar cheese, and sour cream and stir the mixture into the soup. Let stand, covered, for 10 minutes.

5. Stir again and serve, garnished with chopped chives.

Hearty Beef Stew

Yield: Serves 8 | Prep Time: 15 minutes | Cook Time: 8¼ to 10¼ hours on Low or 4¼ to 5¼ hours on High

This Hearty Beef Stew will get you through the worst kinds of weather. Winter can get rough out in the Midwest, so when I hear that a storm is on its way, I stock up on my beef stew essentials and make this warm and cozy favorite to stave off the cold.

INGREDIENTS

2 pounds beef stew meat, cut into 1-inch pieces

1 teaspoon kosher salt

½ teaspoon freshly ground black pepper

4 tablespoons all-purpose flour

1 tablespoon olive oil

1 pound Yukon Gold potatoes, peeled and cut into 1-inch cubes

4 carrots, cut into 1-inch pieces

2 onions, cut into wedges

4 garlic cloves, minced

2½ cups beef broth

1 (6-ounce) can tomato paste

1 (14-ounce) can fire-roasted diced tomatoes

1 tablespoon Worcestershire sauce

1 teaspoon dried thyme

1 bay leaf

1 cup frozen peas, thawed

DIRECTIONS

1. Lightly spray the insert of a 6-quart slow cooker with cooking spray.

2. Season the beef with the salt and pepper. Coat the beef with 2 tablespoons of the flour.

3. In a large skillet, heat the olive oil over medium heat. Add the beef and sear until browned on all sides, 5 to 8 minutes.

4. Place the potatoes, carrots, onions, and garlic in the slow cooker. Top with the browned beef.

5. Add 2 cups of the broth, the tomato paste, diced tomatoes, Worcestershire sauce, thyme, and bay leaf. Stir.

6. Cover and cook on Low for 8 to 10 hours or on High for 4 to 5 hours.

7. Remove the bay leaf.

8. In a small bowl, combine the remaining 2 tablespoons of the flour and ½ cup of the broth and mix well. Stir the flour mixture into the stew and add the peas.

9. Cover and cook on High for 15 minutes more, until the mixture thickens.

10. Ladle into bowls and serve.

Taco Soup

Yield: Serves 6 to 8 | Prep Time: 20 minutes | Cook Time: 6 to 8 hours on Low or 3 to 4 hours on High

Tacos have so many different elements to play with. From the meat to the cheese to the tomatoes to the sour cream, it's like a burst of different flavors melding together in each bite. Now with this soup version, you can throw all those flavors in a thermos and have that delicious taco taste wherever you go.

INGREDIENTS

1 pound ground beef

2 (16-ounce) cans kidney beans, drained and rinsed

1 (15-ounce) can black beans, drained and rinsed

2 (12-ounce) cans Ro-Tel tomatoes

1 (10-ounce) bag frozen corn

1 (10-ounce) can tomato sauce

1 (1-ounce) package taco seasoning mix

1 (1-ounce) package ranch dressing mix

1 (32-ounce) carton chicken broth

Tortilla chips, for serving

Shredded cheddar cheese, for serving

Cilantro, for serving

DIRECTIONS

1. In a large saucepan, brown the beef over medium heat. Drain off the excess fat, then transfer the beef to a 6-quart slow cooker.

2. Add the kidney beans, black beans, Ro-Tel tomatoes, frozen corn, tomato sauce, taco seasoning mix, ranch dressing mix, and broth. Stir to combine.

3. Cook on Low for 6 to 8 hours or on High for 3 to 4 hours.

4. Serve in bowls and top with tortilla chips, cheddar cheese, and cilantro.

7

Dessert Recipes

With all the sauces, sprinkles, and candies to choose from, desserts are where your creativity is truly allowed to shine with the most colorful dishes imaginable. I love these recipes because you can have dinner cooking on the stovetop or in the oven with a surprise dessert simmering and waiting to go in the slow cooker. From fruity hits to decadent chocolate cakes, these desserts will satisfy every craving!

Dump Cake

Yield: Serves 6 to 8 | Prep Time: 10 minutes | Cook Time: 2 hours

Recipes where you can dump all the ingredients into one pot and come back to a finished dish later are the true joy of using a slow cooker. Why do the work when your slow cooker can do it for you? I like to make this sweet treat on a weeknight as a little pick-me-up when I'm pressed for time.

INGREDIENTS

2 (21-ounce) cans apple pie filling

1 (16.25-ounce) box white cake mix

½ cup (1 stick) unsalted butter, melted

Caramel sauce, warmed, for serving

DIRECTIONS

1. Spray the insert of a 6-quart slow cooker with cooking spray.

2. Pour the apple pie filling into the slow cooker and spread it evenly over the bottom.

3. In a medium bowl, combine the cake mix and melted butter and stir until crumbly.

4. Pour the cake crumble mixture over the apple pie filling and spread it out evenly. Cover and cook on High for 2 hours.

5. Scoop into bowls and serve with a drizzle of warm caramel sauce.

Apple Dumplings

Yield: Serves 8 | Prep Time: 20 minutes | Cook Time: 4 to 6 hours

Whenever I go apple picking, I get caught up in the fun and end up picking way more apples than I know what to do with. Then I discovered this recipe for Apple Dumplings, a perfect way to create an easy apple dessert that everyone will love. The lemon-lime soda adds a distinct sweetness to a dish that's already craveable.

INGREDIENTS

3 (8-ounce) cans crescent rolls

3 apples, peeled, cored, and sliced into 8 wedges each

1 cup granulated sugar

½ cup packed light brown sugar

1 tablespoon apple pie spice

1 cup (2 sticks) unsalted butter, cut into ½-tablespoon slices

1 teaspoon vanilla extract

1 (12-ounce) can lemon-lime soda

Caramel sauce, warmed, for serving

DIRECTIONS

1. Spray the insert of a 6-quart slow cooker with cooking spray.

2. Separate the crescent roll dough along the perforations. Wrap one crescent roll around an apple slice starting at the small end of the crescent roll. Place in the slow cooker. Repeat with each apple slice.

3. In a large microwaveable bowl, combine the granulated sugar, brown sugar, and apple pie spice. Arrange the butter slices over the sugar and apple spice mixture. Microwave in 15-second intervals until the butter has fully melted. Mix in the vanilla. Pour the mixture over the apple dumplings.

4. Carefully pour the lemon-lime soda around the edges and between the apple dumplings—not over the top.

5. Cover and cook on High for 4 to 6 hours. The apple dumplings will be puffed up and golden brown.

6. Serve with a drizzle of warm caramel sauce.

Apple Pecan Bread Pudding

Yield: Serves 6 to 8 | Prep Time: 20 minutes | Cook Time: 3 to 4 hours on Low or 2 to 3 hours on High

When I think of fall, I think of this recipe. It has cinnamon, apples, and pecans all rolled into one gooey treat, making it the ultimate cozy dessert for the cool months.

INGREDIENTS

8 slices cinnamon-raisin bread, cut into cubes

2 tart apples, peeled, cored, and diced

1 cup chopped pecans, toasted

½ cup raisins

¾ cup granulated sugar

¼ cup packed light brown sugar

1 teaspoon ground cinnamon

⅛ teaspoon freshly grated nutmeg

3 large eggs, lightly beaten

2 cups half-and-half

¼ cup apple cider

½ teaspoon vanilla extract

¼ teaspoon kosher salt

4 tablespoons (½ stick) unsalted butter, melted

Caramel sauce, warmed, for serving

DIRECTIONS

1. Spray the insert of a 6-quart slow cooker with cooking spray.

2. Place the bread cubes, apples, pecans, and raisins in the slow cooker.

3. In a small bowl, combine the granulated sugar, brown sugar, cinnamon, and nutmeg. Add the eggs, half-and-half, apple cider, vanilla, salt, and melted butter. Mix well to combine. Pour over the bread mixture.

4. Cover and cook on Low for 3 to 4 hours or on High for 2 to 3 hours, until the pudding has set up and a knife inserted into the center comes out clean.

5. Serve with a drizzle of warm caramel sauce.

Berry Crumble

Yield: Serves 4 | Prep Time: 10 minutes | Cook Time: 4 hours

This has "midnight snack" written all over it. I love making it when my friends are coming over for a movie marathon night, and we know we'll need a sweet treat after we've waded through the pretzels and popcorn. This Berry Crumble always hits the spot.

INGREDIENTS

1 (21-ounce) can raspberry pie filling

½ cup quick-cooking oats

½ cup slivered almonds, plus more for garnish

⅔ cup packed light brown sugar

½ cup all-purpose flour

½ cup (1 stick) unsalted butter, cut into pieces, at room temperature

DIRECTIONS

1. Lightly spray the insert of a 6-quart slow cooker with cooking spray.

2. Spread the raspberry pie filling evenly over the bottom of the slow cooker.

3. In a medium bowl, combine the oats, almonds, brown sugar, and flour. Add the butter and cut it in with a pastry blender. Sprinkle the mixture evenly over the pie filling.

4. Cover and cook on Low for 4 hours. The mixture will thicken and bubble when done.

5. Top with additional slivered almonds and serve warm.

VARIATIONS

Try this recipe with another flavored pie filling like lemon, cherry, apple, and more!

Caramel Blondies

Yield: Serves 4 to 6 | Prep Time: 10 minutes | Cook Time: 2½ to 3 hours

I love making these Caramel Blondies for Sunday book club. They're easy to make, but they look like they came from a fancy bakery. Just cut them into squares and store in plastic storage containers to bring them along, and drizzle the caramel sauce on top right before serving.

INGREDIENTS

1 cup all-purpose flour

1 teaspoon baking powder

1¾ teaspoons kosher salt

½ cup packed light brown sugar

4 tablespoons (½ stick) unsalted butter, at room temperature

1 teaspoon vanilla extract

½ cup whole milk

12 soft square caramels (about 3.5 ounces), unwrapped

1 (14-ounce) jar caramel sauce, plus more for serving, warmed

Sugar sprinkles, for garnish

DIRECTIONS

1. Spray the insert of a 4-quart slow cooker with cooking spray.

2. In a medium bowl, combine the flour, baking powder, and ¾ teaspoon of the salt.

3. In another medium bowl, mix together the brown sugar and butter until creamy. Stir in the vanilla.

4. Mix in about half the flour mixture, followed by half the milk. Continue adding the flour and milk, alternating each and beating well after each addition, until you've added all of each. Stir in the caramels.

5. Spread the batter evenly over the bottom of the slow cooker.

6. Pour the caramel sauce into a microwaveable bowl. Microwave for about 1 minute. Carefully stir the remaining 1 teaspoon of salt into the caramel and then pour the caramel over the blondie mixture into the slow cooker.

7. Cover and cook on Low for 2½ to 3 hours.

8. Serve with a drizzle of warm caramel sauce and sugar sprinkles.

Gluten-Free Zucchini Bread

Yield: 1 loaf | Prep Time: 20 minutes | Cook Time: 4 hours

It's so important to me to make sure all my guests feel included, which is why this gluten-free bread is perfect. Your gluten-free friends will be happy to see there's a sweet treat for them, too.

INGREDIENTS

1 zucchini (about 8 ounces)

½ cup walnuts

1½ cups plus 1 tablespoon gluten-free flour, such as King Arthur Gluten-Free Flour

½ cup granulated sugar

½ cup packed light brown sugar

1 teaspoon ground cinnamon

1 teaspoon freshly grated nutmeg

½ cup vegetable oil

2 large eggs

1 teaspoon vanilla extract

½ teaspoon baking soda

¼ teaspoon baking powder

Glaze

½ cup powdered sugar

1 teaspoon lemon zest, plus more for garnish

1½ tablespoons fresh lemon juice

DIRECTIONS

1. Spray a loaf pan with cooking spray. Using a food processor with a shredding blade, shred the zucchini and place 2 cups into a large bowl. Place the walnuts and 1 tablespoon of the gluten-free flour into the same processor bowl, and with the chopping blade pulse until the walnuts are coarsely chopped. Add the walnut mixture to the zucchini and set aside.

2. In the food processor using the chopping blade, combine the sugar, brown sugar, cinnamon, and nutmeg and pulse until well mixed. With the machine running, add the vegetable oil, eggs, and vanilla, pulsing briefly.

3. In a medium bowl, combine the remaining 1½ cups of gluten-free flour, the baking soda, and the baking powder and toss to mix. Add to the food processor. Pulse just until all the dry ingredients are incorporated. Spoon the batter into the bowl with the zucchini mixture and stir by hand until well combined.

4. Spoon the batter into the prepared loaf pan. Spray a piece of aluminum foil with cooking spray and position it, sprayed-side down, on top of the loaf pan. Tightly seal. Place the loaf pan in the slow cooker and carefully add water to a depth of 1 inch around the pan. Cover and cook on High for 4 hours.

5. Carefully remove the loaf pan and let cool on a wire rack for 10 minutes before removing from the pan.

6. *For the glaze:* In a small bowl, stir together the powdered sugar, lemon zest, and lemon juice until well mixed and drizzle over the bread. Cut into slices, garnish with lemon zest, and serve.

Pineapple Upside-Down Cake

Yield: Serves 10 to 12 | Prep Time: 20 minutes | Cook Time: 3 hours

This retro recipe reminds me of the holidays when one of my aunts would always show up with an upside-down cake in hand. It became a reliable comfort, and family get-togethers weren't the same without it. I remember watching as a kid as my aunt flipped it over, and the magical moment when it appeared on the plate in one piece.

INGREDIENTS

1 cup packed light brown sugar

4 tablespoons (½ stick) unsalted butter, melted

1 cup pecans, finely chopped

1 (20-ounce) can pineapple rings in juice, drained, juice reserved

10 maraschino cherries without stems, drained, juice reserved

1 (15.25-ounce) box yellow cake mix

Vegetable oil and eggs as called for on the cake mix box

DIRECTIONS

1. Lightly spray the insert of a 6-quart slow cooker with cooking spray.

2. In a small bowl, combine the brown sugar and melted butter. Spread evenly over the bottom of the slow cooker. Sprinkle the chopped pecans evenly over the sugar mixture. Arrange the pineapple slices on top. Place a maraschino cherry in the center of each pineapple ring.

3. Add enough of the reserved cherry juice to the reserved pineapple juice to measure 1 cup total. Make the cake batter as directed on the box, substituting the pineapple-cherry juice mixture for the water. Pour the batter evenly over the ingredients in the slow cooker.

4. Cook on High for 3 hours, or until a toothpick inserted into the center comes out clean. Uncover the cake and transfer the slow cooker insert to a cooling rack. Let cool for 15 minutes. Avoid waiting any longer, as the sugar will set and make the cake difficult to remove from the slow cooker. Run a sharp knife along the edges of the cake to loosen it from the slow cooker.

5. Place a heatproof serving plate upside down over the top of the slow cooker insert; carefully turn the plate and slow cooker insert over together. The cake will fall onto the plate. If any pineapple slices or cherries stick to the insert, gently remove them and return them to the cake.

6. Serve warm.

Hot Fudge Brownies

Yield: Serves 6 to 8 | Prep Time: 10 minutes | Cook Time: 2½ to 3 hours

Chocoholics won't be able to get enough of this slow cooker dessert favorite because it's oozing with layers of chocolate in every bite.

INGREDIENTS

1 (20-ounce) package brownie mix

Vegetable oil and eggs as called for on the brownie mix box

1 cup chocolate syrup

1 cup hot water

Hot fudge, for topping

Mint candies, for topping

DIRECTIONS

1. Spray the insert of a 6-quart slow cooker with cooking spray.

2. Prepare the brownie batter according to the package directions.

3. Pour the prepared brownie batter into the slow cooker, spreading it evenly.

4. In a medium bowl, whisk together the chocolate syrup and hot water. Pour over the batter.

5. Cover and cook on High for 2½ to 3 hours, until the edges are just beginning to set but not burn.

6. Turn off the slow cooker and remove the lid. Let stand for 30 minutes to allow the middle to set up.

7. Serve with hot fudge and top with mint candies.

Peach Cobbler

Yield: Serves 4 to 6 | Prep Time: 10 minutes | Cook Time: 7 to 9 hours on Low or 4 to 6 hours on High

Make sure you have some vanilla ice cream on hand to serve alongside this warm Southern dessert. The bourbon makes this recipe ideal for a ladies' night in, filled with cocktails, card games, and good conversation.

INGREDIENTS

Peach Filling

3 pounds fresh or frozen peaches, pitted, if fresh, and sliced, plus additioonal for garnish

¾ cup apple butter

¼ cup bourbon

¼ cup sugar

¼ teaspoon kosher salt

Cobbler

1½ cups all-purpose flour

¾ cup yellow cornmeal

¾ cup sugar

1 tablespoon baking powder

1 teaspoon kosher salt

1¼ cups whole milk

½ cup (1 stick) unsalted butter, melted

DIRECTIONS

1. *For the peach filling:* Spray the insert of a 6-quart slow cooker with cooking spray.

2. Place the peaches, apple butter, bourbon, sugar, and salt in the slow cooker. Stir to coat the peaches fully, then spread them out evenly.

3. *For the cobbler:* In a large bowl, mix the flour, yellow cornmeal, sugar, baking powder, and salt. Whisk in the milk. Whisk in the melted butter until smooth. Pour the batter over the peaches, making sure it coats the entire surface.

4. Place a long piece of paper towel over the slow cooker and cover with the lid. Pull the paper towel tight so it doesn't sag. Cook on Low for 7 to 9 hours or on High for 4 to 6 hours, until a toothpick inserted into the center comes out clean. Once the middle of the top has puffed up and is golden around the edges, the peach cobbler is ready to serve.

5. Serve warm, garnished with extra peach slices.

Peanut Butter Cup Cake

Yield: Serves 10 to 12 | Prep Time: 20 minutes | Cook Time: 1½ to 2 hours

Peanut butter and chocolate are one of those combinations that simply work. When you add a fudgy element, it brings the dessert to a whole new level.

INGREDIENTS

Cake

1 (15.25-ounce) box yellow cake mix

3 large eggs

½ cup creamy peanut butter

⅓ cup unsalted butter, at room temperature

½ cup chocolate fudge sauce

Topping

3 tablespoons creamy peanut butter

2 tablespoons whole milk, plus more if necessary

1 cup powdered sugar

2 tablespoons chocolate fudge sauce

8 ounces mini peanut butter cups

¼ cup roasted salted peanuts, coarsely chopped

DIRECTIONS

1. *For the cake:* Lightly spray a 6-quart slow cooker with cooking spray.

2. In the bowl of a stand mixer fitted with the paddle attachment, beat together the yellow cake mix, eggs, peanut butter, butter, and 1 cup of water on low speed for 30 seconds, then on medium speed for 2 minutes, stopping to scrape down the bowl a few times.

3. Warm the fudge sauce in the microwave slightly, just enough that it pours easily.

4. Spoon half the peanut butter batter into the slow cooker, followed by the chocolate fudge sauce, reserving 2 tablespoons of the fudge sauce for the topping. Top with the remaining peanut butter batter. Swirl the batter and fudge sauce together with a knife, but don't mix them entirely.

5. Cover and cook on High for 1½ to 2 hours, or until a toothpick inserted into the center of the cake comes out clean. Transfer the slow cooker insert to a wire rack. Let cool for 15 minutes.

6. Run a sharp knife along the edges of the cake to loosen it from the slow cooker insert. Put a serving platter over the top of the slow cooker insert and invert the platter and insert together so the cake falls out onto the platter.

7. *For the topping:* While the cake cools, beat the peanut butter and milk together in a medium bowl until smooth. Add the powdered sugar and mix until smooth. If necessary, gradually add additional milk until the frosting is the desired consistency.

8. Drizzle the peanut butter frosting over the cake and drizzle with the fudge sauce. Sprinkle the peanut butter cups and chopped peanuts over the top of the cake. Serve.

Old-Fashioned Pecan Pie

Yield: Serves 10 to 12 | Prep Time: 20 minutes | Cook Time: 2½ to 3 hours

The holidays can get pretty jam-packed, especially when it comes to valuable kitchen space. While the main course is in the oven and a couple of different sides are cooking on the stovetop, I like having dessert, like this Old-Fashioned Pecan Pie, warm and ready in the slow cooker. It's an easy way to have an awe-inspiring holiday spread without getting stressed out in the kitchen.

INGREDIENTS

1 refrigerated piecrust

3 large eggs

1 cup sugar

⅔ cup dark corn syrup

⅓ cup unsalted butter, melted

2 tablespoons bourbon

⅛ teaspoon kosher salt

1 teaspoon vanilla extract

1 cup pecans, coarsely chopped, plus ½ cup whole pecans

DIRECTIONS

1. Lightly spray the insert of a 6-quart slow cooker with cooking spray.

2. If your slow cooker is an oval, you'll need to shape the pie dough slightly. On a lightly floured surface, roll the pie dough lightly in one direction to make the circle into an oval slightly larger than the slow cooker. Carefully place the dough in the slow cooker, rolling the excess dough around the edges to make a lip to hold the toppings.

3. In a large bowl, whisk together the eggs, sugar, corn syrup, butter, bourbon, salt, and vanilla until well mixed.

4. Stir in the chopped pecans. Pour the filling into the slow cooker over the pie dough. Gently arrange the whole pecans in a pretty pattern on top of the filling. I like to have a row along the edge of the piecrust and a few more scattered in the middle.

5. Place two long pieces of paper towel over the top of the slow cooker and cover with the lid. Cook on High for 2½ to 3 hours. Transfer the slow cooker insert to a wire rack and let cool for 15 minutes.

6. Serve warm.

Pumpkin Cake

Yield: Serves 6 to 8 | Prep Time: 5 minutes | Cook Time: 2 to 4 hours

When October rolls around, I go into a pumpkin frenzy. Fall is not the same without finding ways to sneak pumpkin into everything. This dish is perfect to prep on a Sunday afternoon before getting dinner ready. Then by the time that's all finished, I'm ready to dive right in.

INGREDIENTS

1 (15-ounce) can pure pumpkin puree

1 (12-ounce) can evaporated milk

¾ cup packed light brown sugar, plus more for garnish

½ cup all-purpose flour

¼ teaspoon kosher salt

½ teaspoon baking powder

2 large eggs, beaten

2 tablespoons unsalted butter, melted

2 teaspoons pumpkin spice

Pecans, for garnish

DIRECTIONS

1. Spray the insert of a 6-quart slow cooker with cooking spray.

2. Combine the pumpkin, evaporated milk, brown sugar, flour, salt, baking powder, eggs, butter, and pumpkin spice in the slow cooker and cook on Low for 2 to 4 hours.

3. Top with brown sugar and pecans and serve.

Acknowledgments

Thank you to my dad, a supportive and strong person. He's always around when I need him and always filled with thoughtful ideas and advice. He is also a great cook.

Thank you to my incredibly culinary and creative team at Prime Publishing.

Megan Von Schönhoff and Tom Krawczyk, my photographers. Chris Hammond, Judith Hines, and Marlene Stolfo, my culinary test kitchen geniuses. To word masters and editors Bryn Clark, Elizabeth Curione, and Jessica Thelander. To Brant Janeway, Erica Martirano, Jaclyn Waggner, and Justine Sha, thank you for helping to get these books out in the world and into the hands of home cooks everywhere. And to my amazing editor and friend, Kara Rota. This book was a team effort, filled with collaboration and creativity that reached no limits.

Index

Alfredo, Chicken Broccoli, 111
almond(s)
    Berry Crumble, 204
appetizers
    Bacon Cheeseburger Dip, 5
    Bacon-Wrapped Smokies, 6
    Barbecue Meatballs, 9
    Beer and Brown Sugar Kielbasa, 10
    Buffalo Wings, 13
    Honey Buffalo Chicken Sliders, 21
    Queso Blanco, 18
    7-Layer Dip, 25
    Shredded Chicken Nachos, 22
    Spinach Artichoke Dip, 26
    Sweet-and-Savory Party Mix, 17
apple(s)
    Apple Dumplings, 200
    Apple Pecan Bread Pudding, 203
    Dump Cake, 199
Artichoke Spinach Dip, 26
Artisan Bread, Easy, 51
Au Gratin Potatoes, 151

baby back ribs
    Sweet Sesame Ribs, 80
bacon
    Bacon Cheeseburger Dip, 5
    Bacon-Wrapped Smokies, 6
    Easy Quiche, 43
    Ranch Bacon Chicken Dinner, 128
baguettes
    Banana French Toast, 31
    French Dip Sandwiches, 96
Baked Potatoes, DIY, 152
Baked Ziti, 95
bamboo shoots
    Soba Noodles with Vegetables, 119
Banana French Toast, 31

banana(s)
    Banana French Toast, 31
    Chocolate Chip Banana Bread, 48
Barbecue Meatballs, 9
bean(s)
    Budget-Friendly Chicken Stew, 182
    Chicken Tortilla Soup, 181
    Chili, 63
    Country-Style Baked Beans, 163
    Minestrone Pasta, 186
    Ranch Bacon Chicken Dinner, 128
    7-Layer Dip, 25
    Shredded Chicken Nachos, 22
    Stuffed Peppers, 87
    Taco Soup, 194
beef
    Bacon Cheeseburger Dip, 5
    Barbecue Meatballs, 9
    Beef and Broccoli, 136
    Beef Stroganoff, 59
    Cheeseburger Soup, 185
    Chili, 63
    Corned Beef and Cabbage, 67
    French Dip Sandwiches, 96
    Hearty Beef Stew, 193
    Hungarian Goulash, 189
    Philly Cheesesteaks, 112
    Potato Puff Casserole, 104
    Ritz Cracker Meat Loaf, 72
    From-Scratch Italian Lasagna, 71
    Taco Soup, 194
Beer and Brown Sugar Kielbasa, 10
Berry Crumble, 204
black beans
    Chicken Tortilla Soup, 181
    Stuffed Peppers, 87
    Taco Soup, 194
Blondies, Caramel, 207
Blueberry Breakfast Casserole, 32

Bourbon Chicken, 116
bread
    Banana French Toast, 31
    Chocolate Chip French Toast, 35
    Corn Bread, 168
    Dinner Rolls, 172
    Easy Artisan Bread, 51
    Gluten-Free Zucchini Bread, 208
    Lemon Poppy Seed Bread, 52
    Monkey Bread, 55
    Pizza Pull-Apart Bread, 171
    Slow Cooker Stuffing, 167
Bread Pudding, Apple Pecan, 203
breakfasts
    Banana French Toast, 31
    Blueberry Breakfast Casserole, 32
    Chocolate Chip Banana Bread, 48
    Chocolate Chip French Toast, 35
    Cinnamon Rolls, 39
    Coffee Cake, 40
    Easy Artisan Bread, 51
    Easy Quiche, 43
    Lemon Poppy Seed Bread, 52
    Monkey Bread, 55
    Potato Puff Breakfast Casserole, 47
    Sausage and Hash Brown
        Casserole, 35
    Veggie Omelet, 44
brisket
    Corned Beef and Cabbage, 67
broccoli
    Beef and Broccoli, 136
    Chicken Broccoli Alfredo, 111
    Honey Mustard Chicken and
        Broccoli, 140
brownies
    Caramel Blondies, 207
    Hot Fudge Brownies, 212
Budget-Friendly Chicken Stew, 182

Buffalo Chicken Sandwiches, 64
Buffalo Wings, 13
butter beans
    Country-Style Baked Beans, 163
Buttery Corn on the Cob, 155

Cabbage, Corned Beef and, 67
Caesar Chicken, 107
cakes
    Coffee Cake, 40
    Dump Cake, 199
    Peanut Butter Cup Cake, 216
    Pineapple Upside-Down Cake, 211
    Pumpkin Cake, 220
Caramel Blondies, 207
carrot(s)
    Chicken Noodle Soup, 178
    Hearty Beef Stew, 193
    Honey-Glazed Carrots, 160
    Melt-in-Your Mouth Pot Roast, 76
    Soba Noodles with
        Vegetables, 119
cashews
    Sweet-and-Savory Party Mix, 17
casseroles
    Blueberry Breakfast Casserole, 32
    Pierogi Casserole with Sausage, 115
    Potato Puff Breakfast
        Casserole, 47
    Potato Puff Casserole, 104
    Sausage and Hash Brown
        Casserole, 35
    Tuna Casserole, 91
cereals
    Sweet-and-Savory Party Mix, 17
challah bread
    Chocolate Chip French Toast, 35
cheddar cheese
    Cheesy Chicken and Rice, 108
    Ham and Cheese Potatoes, 100
    Mac 'n' Cheese, 164
    Pierogi Casserole with Sausage, 115
    Potato Puff Breakfast Casserole, 47
    Potato Puff Casserole, 104
    Potato Soup, 190
    Sausage and Hash Brown
        Casserole, 35
    Stuffed Peppers, 87
    Tuna Casserole, 91
    Veggie Omelet, 44

cheese
    Bacon Cheeseburger Dip, 5
    Baked Ziti, 95
    Caesar Chicken, 107
    Cheeseburger Soup, 185
    Cheesy Chicken and Rice, 108
    Chicken Broccoli Alfredo, 111
    Chicken Cordon Bleu, 75
    Chicken Parmesan, 60
    Creamed Corn, 156
    Creamy Mashed Potatoes, 159
    Easy Quiche, 43
    4-Cheese Vegetarian Eggplant
        Parmesan, 68
    French Onion Soup, 177
    Ham and Cheese Potatoes, 100
    Mac 'n' Cheese, 164
    Minestrone Pasta, 186
    Parmesan Ranch Oyster
        Crackers, 14
    Philly Cheesesteaks, 112
    Pierogi Casserole with Sausage, 115
    Pizza Pull-Apart Bread, 171
    Potato Puff Breakfast Casserole, 47
    Potato Puff Casserole, 104
    Potato Soup, 190
    Queso Blanco, 18
    Sausage and Hash Brown
        Casserole, 35
    From-Scratch Italian Lasagna, 71
    7-Layer Dip, 25
    Shredded Chicken Nachos, 22
    Spinach Artichoke Dip, 26
    Stuffed Peppers, 87
    Tuna Casserole, 91
    Veggie Omelet, 44
Cheeseburger Soup, 185
Cheesy Chicken and Rice, 108
cherry(ies)
    Pineapple Upside-Down Cake, 211
chicken
    Bourbon Chicken, 116
    Budget-Friendly Chicken Stew, 182
    Buffalo Chicken Sandwiches, 64
    Buffalo Wings, 13
    Caesar Chicken, 107
    Cheesy Chicken and Rice, 108
    Chicken Broccoli Alfredo, 111
    Chicken Cordon Bleu, 75
    Chicken Fried Rice, 139
    Chicken Noodle Soup, 178

    Chicken Parmesan, 60
    Chicken Tortilla Soup, 181
    General Tso's Chicken, 123
    Honey Buffalo Chicken Sliders, 21
    Honey Mustard Chicken and
        Broccoli, 140
    Jambalaya, 103
    Lemon Pepper Chicken Breasts, 88
    Melt-in-Your Mouth Pot Roast, 76
    Mississippi Chicken, 124
    Orange Chicken, 127
    Ranch Bacon Chicken Dinner, 128
    Roasted Chicken, 83
    Shredded Chicken Nachos, 22
    Shredded Chicken Tacos, 144
    6-Ingredient Sriracha Chicken, 135
    Slow Cooker Chicken Breast with
        Stuffing, 132
    Soba Noodles with Vegetables, 119
    Teriyaki Chicken, 147
chili
    Chili, 63
    7-Layer Dip, 25
chili beans
    Country-Style Baked Beans, 163
chocolate chips
    Chocolate Chip Banana
        Bread, 48
    Chocolate Chip French Toast, 35
chuck roast
    Beef and Broccoli, 136
    Beef Stroganoff, 59
    French Dip Sandwiches, 96
    Philly Cheesesteaks, 112
Cinnamon Rolls, 39
Cobbler, Peach, 215
cocktail links
    Bacon-Wrapped Smokies, 6
Coffee Cake, 40
Colby Jack cheese
    Sausage and Hash Brown
        Casserole, 35
corn
    Buttery Corn on the Cob, 155
    Cheesy Chicken and Rice, 108
    Chicken Tortilla Soup, 181
    Corn Bread, 168
    Creamed Corn, 156
    Queso Blanco, 18
    Soba Noodles with Vegetables, 119
    Stuffed Peppers, 87

Corned Beef and Cabbage, 67
Country-Style Baked Beans, 163
cream cheese
    Creamed Corn, 156
    Creamy Mashed Potatoes, 159
    Pierogi Casserole with Sausage, 115
    Queso Blanco, 18
    7-Layer Dip, 25
creamed corn
    Creamed Corn, 156
    Queso Blanco, 18
Creamy Mashed Potatoes, 159
crescent rolls
    Apple Dumplings, 200
Crumble, Berry, 204

desserts
    Apple Dumplings, 200
    Apple Pecan Bread Pudding, 203
    Berry Crumble, 204
    Caramel Blondies, 207
    Chocolate Chip Banana Bread, 48
    Dump Cake, 199
    Gluten-Free Zucchini Bread, 208
    Hot Fudge Brownies, 212
    Old-Fashioned Pecan Pie, 219
    Peach Cobbler, 215
    Peanut Butter Cup Cake, 216
    Pineapple Upside-Down
        Cake, 211
    Pumpkin Cake, 220
Dinner Rolls, 172
dinners
    Baked Ziti, 95
    Beef and Broccoli, 136
    Beef Stroganoff, 59
    Bourbon Chicken, 116
    Buffalo Chicken Sandwiches, 64
    Caesar Chicken, 107
    Cheesy Chicken and Rice, 108
    Chicken and Fried Rice, 139
    Chicken Broccoli Alfredo, 111
    Chicken Cordon Bleu, 73
    Chicken Parmesan, 60
    Chili, 63
    Corned Beef and Cabbage, 67
    4-Cheese Vegetarian Eggplant
        Parmesan, 68
    French Dip Sandwiches, 96
    French Onion Pork Chops, 131

General Tso's Chicken, 123
Ham and Cheese Potatoes, 100
Honey Mustard Chicken and
    Broccoli, 140
Jambalaya, 103
Lemon Pepper Chicken
    Breasts, 88
Lemon Pepper Salmon, 143
Melt-in-Your-Mouth Pot Roast, 76
Mississippi Chicken, 124
Orange Chicken, 127
Philly Cheesesteaks, 112
Pierogi Casserole with Sausage, 115
Potato Puff Casserole, 104
Pulled Pork, 79
Ranch Bacon Chicken Dinner, 128
Ritz Cracker Meat Loaf, 72
Roasted Chicken, 83
From-Scratch Italian Lasagna, 71
Shredded Chicken Tacos, 144
6-Ingredient Sriracha Chicken, 135
Slow Cooker Chicken Breast with
    Stuffing, 132
Slow Cooker Pork Chops, 120
Smothered Pork Chops in
    Mushroom Sauce, 84
Stuffed Peppers, 87
Sweet Pineapple Ham, 99
Sweet Sesame Ribs, 80
Teriyaki Chicken, 147
Tuna Casserole, 91
DIY Baked Potatoes, 152
Dump Cake, 199
Dumplings, Apple, 200

Easy Artisan Bread, 51
egg noodles
    Beef Stroganoff, 59
    Chicken Noodle Soup, 178
    Hungarian Goulash, 189
    Tuna Casserole, 91
Eggplant Parmesan, 4-Cheese
    Vegetarian, 68
egg(s)
    Banana French Toast, 31
    Chicken Tortilla Soup, 181
    Chocolate Chip French Toast, 35
    Easy Quiche, 43
    Potato Puff Breakfast Casserole, 47
    Potato Puff Casserole, 104

Sausage and Hash Brown
    Casserole, 35
Soba Noodles with Vegetables, 119
Veggie Omelet, 44

fish
    Lemon Pepper Salmon, 143
    Tuna Casserole, 91
4-Cheese Vegetarian Eggplant
    Parmesan, 68
French Dip Sandwiches, 96
French Onion Pork Chops, 131
French Onion Soup, 177
French toast
    Banana French Toast, 31
    Chocolate Chip French Toast, 35
From-Scratch Italian Lasagna, 71

General Tso's Chicken, 123
Gluten-Free Zucchini Bread, 208
Goulash, Hungarian, 189
great northern beans
    Minestrone Pasta, 186
green beans
    Ranch Bacon Chicken Dinner, 128
Gruyère cheese
    Easy Quiche, 43
    French Onion Soup, 177

ham
    Chicken Cordon Bleu, 75
    Ham and Cheese Potatoes, 100
    Sweet Pineapple Ham, 99
Ham and Cheese Potatoes, 100
Hash Brown and Sausage
    Casserole, 35
Hearty Beef Stew, 193
Honey Buffalo Chicken Sliders, 21
Honey Mustard Chicken and
    Broccoli, 140
Honey-Glazed Carrots, 160
Hot Fudge Brownies, 212
Hungarian Goulash, 189

Jambalaya, 103
Jarlsberg cheese
    Chicken Cordon Bleu, 75

kidney beans
    Budget-Friendly Chicken Stew, 182
    Chili, 63
    Minestrone Pasta, 186
    Taco Soup, 194
kielbasa
    Beer and Brown Sugar Kielbasa, 10
    Pierogi Casserole with Sausage, 115

Lasagna, From-Scratch Italian, 71
lemon(s)
    Lemon Pepper Chicken Breasts, 88
    Lemon Pepper Salmon, 143
    Lemon Poppy Seed Bread, 52

Mac 'n' Cheese, 164
Mashed Potatoes, Creamy, 159
Meatballs, Barbecue, 9
Melt-in-Your-Mouth Pot Roast, 76
Minestrone Pasta, 186
Mississippi Chicken, 124
Monkey Bread, 55
mozzarella cheese
    Chicken Parmesan, 60
    4-Cheese Vegetarian Eggplant
        Parmesan, 68
    From-Scratch Italian Lasagna, 71
    Pizza Pull-Apart Bread, 171
    Queso Blanco, 18
    Spinach Artichoke Dip, 26
Muenster cheese
    Ham and Cheese Potatoes, 100
mushroom(s)
    Beef Stroganoff, 59
    Slow Cooker Pork Chops, 120
    Smothered Pork Chops in
        Mushroom Sauce, 84
    Soba Noodles with Vegetables, 119
    Veggie Omelet, 44

Nachos, Shredded Chicken, 22
navy beans
    Country-Style Baked Beans, 163

oats
    Berry Crumble, 204
    Blueberry Breakfast Casserole, 32

Old-Fashioned Pecan Pie, 219
Omelet, Veggie, 44
Orange Chicken, 127
Oyster Crackers, Parmesan Ranch, 14

Parmesan cheese
    Baked Ziti, 95
    Caesar Chicken, 107
    Chicken Broccoli Alfredo, 111
    4-Cheese Vegetarian Eggplant
        Parmesan, 68
    From-Scratch Italian Lasagna, 71
    Mac 'n' Cheese, 164
    Minestrone Pasta, 186
    Parmesan Ranch Oyster
        Crackers, 14
    Pizza Pull-Apart Bread, 171
    Spinach Artichoke Dip, 26
Party Mix, Sweet-and-Savory, 17
pasta
    Baked Ziti, 95
    Beef Stroganoff, 59
    Chicken Broccoli Alfredo, 111
    Chicken Noodle Soup, 178
    Chicken Parmesan, 60
    From-Scratch Italian Lasagna, 71
    Hungarian Goulash, 189
    Mac 'n' Cheese, 164
    Minestrone Pasta, 186
    Soba Noodles with Vegetables, 119
    Tuna Casserole, 91
Peach Cobbler, 215
Peanut Butter Cup Cake, 216
peanuts
    Sweet-and-Savory Party Mix, 17
pecan(s)
    Apple Pecan Bread Pudding, 203
    Old-Fashioned Pecan Pie, 219
    Pineapple Upside-Down
        Cake, 211
pepperoncini
    Mississippi Chicken, 124
pepperoni
    Pizza Pull-Apart Bread, 171
pepper(s)
    Chili, 63
    Philly Cheesesteaks, 112
    Ritz Cracker Meat Loaf, 72
    6-Ingredient Sriracha Chicken, 135
    Stuffed Peppers, 87

Teriyaki Chicken, 147
    Veggie Omelet, 44
Philly Cheesesteaks, 112
Pie, Old-Fashioned Pecan, 219
Pierogi Casserole with Sausage, 115
pineapple(s)
    Bourbon Chicken, 116
    Pineapple Upside-Down Cake, 211
    Sweet Pineapple Ham, 99
    Teriyaki Chicken, 147
pinto beans
    Chili, 63
Pizza Pull-Apart Bread, 171
Poppy Seed Lemon Bread, 52
pork
    Barbecue Meatballs, 9
    Country-Style Baked Beans, 163
    French Onion Pork Chops, 131
    Pulled Pork, 79
    Slow Cooker Pork Chops, 120
    Smothered Pork Chops in
        Mushroom Sauce, 84
    Sweet Sesame Ribs, 80
Pot Roast, Melt-in-Your-Mouth, 76
potato puffs
    Potato Puff Breakfast Casserole, 47
    Potato Puff Casserole, 104
potato(es)
    Au Gratin Potatoes, 151
    Cheeseburger Soup, 185
    Creamy Mashed Potatoes, 159
    DIY Baked Potatoes, 152
    Ham and Cheese Potatoes, 100
    Hearty Beef Stew, 193
    Hungarian Goulash, 189
    Melt-in-Your Mouth Pot Roast, 76
    Pierogi Casserole with
        Sausage, 115
    Potato Puff Breakfast Casserole, 47
    Potato Puff Casserole, 104
    Potato Soup, 190
    Ranch Bacon Chicken Dinner, 128
    Sausage and Hash Brown
        Casserole, 35
pretzels
    Sweet-and-Savory Party Mix, 17
provolone cheese
    4-Cheese Vegetarian Eggplant
        Parmesan, 68
    Philly Cheesesteaks, 112
Pull-Apart Pizza Bread, 171

Pulled Pork, 79
Pumpkin Cake, 220

Queso Blanco, 18
Quiche, Easy, 43
quinoa
    Teriyaki Chicken, 147

raisin bread
    Apple Pecan Bread Pudding, 203
Ranch Bacon Chicken Dinner, 128
raspberry(ies)
    Berry Crumble, 204
refrigerated rolls
    Monkey Bread, 55
    Pizza Pull-Apart Bread, 171
Ribs, Sweet Sesame, 80
rice
    Beef and Broccoli, 136
    Bourbon Chicken, 116
    Cheesy Chicken and Rice, 108
    Chicken Fried Rice, 139
    General Tso's Chicken, 123
    Jambalaya, 103
    Mississippi Chicken, 124
    Orange Chicken, 127
    6-Ingredient Sriracha Chicken, 135
    Stuffed Peppers, 87
    Teriyaki Chicken, 147
ricotta cheese
    Baked Ziti, 95
    4-Cheese Vegetarian Eggplant
        Parmesan, 68
    From-Scratch Italian Lasagna, 71
rigatoni pasta
    Baked Ziti, 95
    Chicken Broccoli Alfredo, 111
Ritz Cracker Meat Loaf, 72
Roasted Chicken, 83

Salmon, Lemon Pepper, 143
salsa
    Shredded Chicken Nachos, 22
sandwiches
    Buffalo Chicken Sandwiches, 64
    French Dip Sandwiches, 96
    Honey Buffalo Chicken Sliders, 21
    Philly Cheesesteaks, 112

sauerkraut
    Beer and Brown Sugar Kielbasa, 10
sausage
    Bacon-Wrapped Smokies, 6
    From-Scratch Italian Lasagna, 71
    Jambalaya, 103
    Pierogi Casserole with Sausage, 115
    Sausage and Hash Brown
        Casserole, 35
Sesame Ribs, Sweet, 80
7-Layer Dip, 25
Shredded Chicken Nachos, 22
Shredded Chicken Tacos, 144
shrimp
    Jambalaya, 103
side dishes
    Au Gratin Potatoes, 151
    Buttery Corn on the Cob, 155
    Corn Bread, 168
    Country-Style Baked Beans, 163
    Creamed Corn, 156
    Creamy Mashed Potatoes, 159
    Dinner Rolls, 172
    DIY Baked Potatoes, 152
    Honey-Glazed Carrots, 160
    Mac 'n' Cheese, 164
    Pizza Pull-Apart Bread, 171
    Slow Cooker Stuffing, 167
6-Ingredient Sriracha Chicken, 135
Sliders, Honey Buffalo Chicken, 21
Slow Cooker Chicken Breast with
    Stuffing, 132
Slow Cooker Pork Chops, 120
Slow Cooker Stuffing, 167
Smothered Pork Chops in Mushroom
    Sauce, 84
Soba Noodles with Vegetables, 119
soups
    Cheeseburger Soup, 185
    Chicken Noodle Soup, 178
    Chicken Tortilla Soup, 181
    French Onion Soup, 177
    Minestrone Pasta, 186
    Potato Soup, 190
    Taco Soup, 194
spaghetti
    Chicken Parmesan, 60
spinach
    Easy Quiche, 43
    Spinach Artichoke Dip, 26
Sriracha Chicken, 6-Ingredient, 135

stews
    Budget-Friendly Chicken
        Stew, 182
    Hearty Beef Stew, 193
    Hungarian Goulash, 189
Stroganoff, Beef, 59
Stuffed Peppers, 87
Stuffing, Slow Cooker, 167
Sweet Pineapple Ham, 99
Sweet Sesame Ribs, 80
Sweet-and-Savory Party Mix, 17

Taco Soup, 194
Tacos, Shredded Chicken, 144
Teriyaki Chicken, 147
tomato(es)
    Chicken Parmesan, 60
    Chicken Tortilla Soup, 181
    Chili, 63
    From-Scratch Italian Lasagna, 71
    Hearty Beef Stew, 193
    Jambalaya, 103
    Minestrone Pasta, 186
    Shredded Chicken Nachos, 22
    Shredded Chicken Tacos, 144
    Stuffed Peppers, 87
    Taco Soup, 194
Tuna Casserole, 91
turkey
    Bacon Cheeseburger Dip, 5
    Potato Puff Breakfast Casserole, 47
    Potato Puff Casserole, 104
    Stuffed Peppers, 87

Vegetarian Eggplant Parmesan,
    4-Cheese, 68
Veggie Omelet, 44
Velveeta cheese
    Cheeseburger Soup, 185
    Mac 'n' Cheese, 164

Wings, Buffalo, 13

Ziti, Baked, 95
zucchini
    Gluten-Free Zucchini Bread, 208
    Veggie Omelet, 44

About the Author

After receiving her master's in culinary arts at Auguste Escoffier in Avignon, France, Addie stayed in France to learn from Christian Etienne at his three-Michelin-star restaurant. Upon leaving France, she spent the next several years working with restaurant groups. She worked in the kitchen for Daniel Boulud and moved coast-to-coast with Thomas Keller building a career in management, restaurant openings, and brand development. She later joined Martha Stewart Living Omnimedia, where she worked with the editorial team as well as in marketing and sales. While living in New York, Addie completed her bachelor's degree in organizational behavior. Upon leaving New York, Addie joined gravitytank, an innovation consultancy in Chicago. As a culinary designer at gravitytank, Addie designed new food products for companies, large and small. She created edible prototypes for clients and research participants to taste and experience, some of which you may see in stores today. In 2015, she debuted on the Food Network, where she competed on *Cutthroat Kitchen*, and won!

Addie is the executive producer for RecipeLion. Addie oversees and creates culinary content for multiple web platforms and communities, leads video strategy, and oversees the production of in-print books. Addie is passionate about taking easy recipes and making them elegant, without making them complicated. From fine dining to entertaining, to innovation and test kitchens, Addie's experience with food makes these recipes unique and delicious.

Addie and her husband live in Lake Forest, Illinois, with their baby boy and happy puppy, Paisley. Addie is actively involved with youth culinary programs in the Chicagoland area, serving on the board of a bakery and catering company that employs at-risk youth. She is a healthy-food teacher for first-graders in a low-income school district, and aside from eating and entertaining with friends and family, she loves encouraging kids to be creative in the kitchen!